the

Suit

COLLINS
An Imprint of HarperCollinsPublishers

the

Suit

A Machiavellian Approach to Men's Style

NICHOLAS ANTONGIAVANNI

HarperCollins books may be purchased for educational, business,
or sales promotional use. For information, please write to:
Special Markets Department, HarperCollins Publishers,
10 East 53rd Street, New York, NY 10022.

Designed by Claire Vaccaro

Library of Congress Cataloging-in-Publication Data has been applied for.

ISBN-10: 0-06-089186-6
ISBN-13: 978-0-06-089186-2

08   09   10   DIX/RRD   10   9   8   7   6   5   4   3   2

Grateful acknowledgment is made to

NICCOLÒ MACHIAVELLI

whose grandeur of vision, intrepidity of thought,

and graceful subtlety of speech served as both

the inspiration and template for this work; to

HARVEY C. MANSFIELD, JR.

without whose graceful, subtle translation

of *The Prince*, the present study could

never have been executed; and

to the learned members of

THE LONDON LOUNGE,

ASK ANDY ABOUT CLOTHES,

and *THE STYLE FORUM,*

whose invaluable discourses on the subject of style helped to

refine much of the sartorial wisdom that informs this book.

Special thanks to:

MICHAEL ALDEN, JAN ANG, AAKASH BHASIN, BEN BOYCHUK,
G. BRUCE BOYER, ALAN CORNETT, JOHN CUSEY, DAVID DESROSIERS,
DAVID ELLIS, CHRISTOPHER FLANNERY, ALAN FLUSSER, CHARLES FRANKE,
TONY GAZIANO, ANDY GILCHRIST, ANDREW HARRIS, EDWARD W. HAYES,
ROLF HOLZAPFEL, JEREMY JACKSON, ALEXANDER KABBAZ,
BRIAN KENNEDY, CHARLES KESLER, DOV KLEINER, LEONARD LOGSDAIL,
MARION MANEKER, MATHEW A. MATHEW, DOUGAL MUNRO, KALEV PEHME,
JULIE PONZI, MATTHEW REES, MARK RYKKEN, RAFE SAGALYN,
ADNAN SALEEM, CATHERINE UY, TITO VARGAS, AND LEAH WARNER

Contents

Contents

Men in general judge more by their

eyes than by their hands,

because seeing is given to everyone,

touching to few.

Everyone sees how you appear,

few touch what you are.

· MACHIAVELLI, *The Prince*, CH. XVIII ·

Dedicatory Letter

Nicholas Antongiavanni to John Elkann:

It is customary for those who desire to acquire favor with a well-dressed man to give him things of their own that they care for most or things that they see please him most. Thus, one often sees them being presented with French lisle socks, English suspenders with white gut ends, bolts of ancient tweed, antique cufflinks, and similar ornaments worthy of their smartness. Since I desire to ask a favor of you with some testimony of my homage to you, I have found nothing in my belongings that I care for so much and esteem so greatly as my knowledge of the habits of well-dressed men, learned from long experience with modern dress and a continuous study of classic style. Having thought out and examined these things with great diligence for a long time, and now reduced them to one small volume, I send it to you.

I hope that you will find it useful in instilling sartorial discipline in your workforce, from which great advantage may be gained. For in times of prosperity, customs and mores always slacken, as success makes men insolent and riches make them idle. But in times of trouble they become circumspect, fretting that their prior conduct has caused their present ruin. They begin to respect those whose habits remained firm even in the boom years. This happens no less in matters of dress, which are an outward sign of our inner spirit. "Business casual" said to the world that making money is so easy, any slob can do it. But now that it has been proved difficult, men are less willing to trust their money to those who do not dress with care and respect. Thus by attiring your company smartly, you would attract all the capital, and overwhelm your competition.

You should aim for them to emulate the dandies of old, while honoring the conventions of our time. And you should not have any fear of the word. As invented by George Brummell two centuries ago, the dandy is the enemy of the splendiferous and effeminate. He instead favors simple clothes, pristine in cut, immaculate in fit, made from resilient materials by expert craftsmen, never ostentatious, always manly—not the garishness of Carson Kressley but the tastefulness of Brian Williams. So far from frippery, dandyism is the mean between foppishness and slovenliness. As Tully says, "in the matter of dress, the intermediate course is best." This little book will help you and your employees find the middle way and thrive along it. And I hope that it will not be thought presumption if a poor and obscure man dares to discuss and give rules for the art of dress. For although looking smart is so much more important for busy global executives than it is for the rest of us, they have no time to study these things, whereas I have had ample occasion to investigate and record them.

Therefore, take this small gift in the spirit with which I send it. If you consider and read it diligently, you will learn from it my extreme desire that you and your employees attain the peak of elegance. And if you will at some time turn your eyes from the summit of the Chairman's suite at Fiat to these low places, you will learn how great is my desire to serve as a sartorial consultant to your company.

I.

How Many Are the Kinds
of Bodies and in What Modes
They Should Be Attired

All human male bodies have been and are either diminutive, of medium height, or tall; and slender, muscular, or stout. Their looking good is caused either by fortune or by virtue. But since Lady Fortune's powers are unfortunately beyond our control, our natural appearance may be pleasing or not according to her whims. And even if it is, necessity and convention require that we adorn ourselves with clothing, and this may be done well or badly. Thus a man must have recourse to his own virtue if he is to look presentable on all occasions; and this virtue consists of the exercise of the body and of the mind. Since tailored clothing can make a man look either rakish or ridiculous, as well as shorter or taller or fatter or thinner, it is necessary for him to choose models, fabrics, and patterns that flatter his shape while minimizing its defects. As Xenophon wrote in his life of Cyrus, it is not reasonable that a big man wear a little coat, or a small man wear a big coat, and expect to look smart.

II.

Of Average Men

I shall leave out reasoning on exercising the body, since that has been treated at length by others. I will discuss only the exercise of the mind, by learning which clothes best suit which forms, and shall proceed by weaving together the threads mentioned above; and I shall debate how these bodies may be attired to look their best.

I say, then, that men of average height and build can wear whatever they want. Nonetheless, the rules discussed below apply to them especially, because their commonness makes them less able to carry off eccentricities of detail. But in terms of fabric, pattern, and model, their choices are limited only by the occasion. Thus the average man should feel free, like Bryant Gumbel, to wear linens in the summer, flannels in the winter, glen plaids during the day, and chalk stripes in the evening; he may choose single- or double-breasted jackets, button down or spread collar shirts, and lace-up or slip-on shoes. He should only contrive to avoid looking ridiculous, as was said.

III.

Of Diminutive Men

But the difficulties reside for all those who are not average. I begin with the diminutive man, who wishes to look taller. The universally recommended modes are to wear only suits made of smooth worsted cloth and to avoid patterns. For flannels and tweeds are bulky and thus make one look wider rather than taller; and plaids do the same by emphasizing horizontal lines. Because they encourage people's eyes to move up and down, stripes are recommended for the diminutive man, provided they are not too far apart—no more than three-quarters of an inch for suits and closer for shirts. Solids should also be a staple of the diminutive man's wardrobe, as they make him look slimmer and thus taller. And diminutive men always look better in suits than in odd jackets and trousers, because the latter cut him in half visually whereas the former present a unified vertical line. As to neckwear, solids elongate best, discreet stripes and small patterns can be worn without harm, and ties wider than three and a half inches should be avoided.

For an example, there is Ross Perot, who attires his tiny frame only in dark worsteds—either solid or striped—always in a solid shirt, and usually in a striped tie. Fortunately for him, the dress codes of both business and politics coincide exactly with those modes most often recommended for the diminutive.

But others have shown greater virtue in attiring themselves. Edward G. Robinson, James Cagney, and Alan Ladd always wore suits with as little superfluous cloth as they could bear, because bagginess adds width, which undermines height. Their jackets (and here I am following the American and Italian usage, whereas English tailors call this garment a coat) were short, because the longer his jacket, the shorter a diminutive man looks, much of his legs being lost under the extra cloth. Reason requires of every man that his jacket always cover his seat lest his clothes look feminine; in the case of the diminutive man, it must extend no farther. Its sleeves should always show a smidgen of shirt cuff (or "linen," as some tailors like to say), for overlong sleeves make him look like a boy wearing his father's overcoat, and he will not be taken seriously; but he should show less than most men—no more than three-eighths of an inch—lest he appear to have outgrown the suit. Jackets should be nipped in at the waist rather than hang straight, and the waist and buttoning point should be high— slightly less than halfway up from the bottom of the jacket. Higher shoulder pads are an absolute boon to the diminutive man, because the raised collar and shoulderline increase the sense of height more than any other mode. When the lapel notches are also placed high, so much the better. Single-breasted jackets whose front edges below the waist button flare outward, forming "open quarters," also help lengthen the leg line, provided the trousers are worn at the natural waist so that no shirt front shows between the waistband and the jacket's waist button. And the diminutive man should always wear his trousers at the natural waist—that is, so that they fasten at the belly button or above. This elongates the appearance of the legs and shortens the torso, adding yet more to the illusion of height. The trouser legs should be just long enough to touch your shoes; any longer and they will look like your older brother's.

And if you consider these things carefully and observe them in the films of Cagney and Ladd, or in *Frazier* co-star David Hyde Pierce, you will see that, though diminutive, they never appeared distractingly short but always well proportioned and elegant—even when wearing cloths other than solid or striped worsteds. For they knew that pattern harms the diminutive man more than cloth—that a plaid sports jacket hurts him far more than a flannel suit; and that patterns whose vertical aspect dominates the horizontal, such as herringbone, harm him hardly at all.

Turning to the other modes, some maintain that the diminutive man's jacket should have side vents, because their vertical lines "move the observer's eye up from the bottom of the jacket"; others insist that side vents widen at least as much as they elongate and advocate a center vent; while still others forbid vents altogether. And surely the latter are correct. For ventless jackets are best at making him look taller, as they are the most slimming.

Opinion is universal with regard to cuffs and pockets. Diminutive men should wear cuffless trousers, because their spareness and smidgen of extra length (for when properly finished they slant downward from front to rear and reach almost to the heel of your shoe yet without puddling) make the legs seem longer, and thus the man taller. They should also wear jackets with flapless (or "besom") pockets, because these are sleeker. Setting the breast pocket a bit higher than normal on the jacket, and the hip pockets a bit lower, also helps to lengthen the silhouette.

Some recommend three-button jackets for the diminutive man, saying that the longer button line emphasizes the vertical. Others recommend two, arguing that longer lapels do the same whereas the shorter lapels of a three-button make him look like a sawed-off Oliver Hardy. Most elongating of all would be the one-button jacket—a specialty of certain Savile Row firms—because in not having the idle bottom button and buttonhole, it is less cluttered. Yet it is more formal and dandified, and also rare, and so not useful for most men, which leaves them with the choice between two or three buttons. And you should know that there are three kinds of three-button jackets: the true three-button, on which the top two buttons are meant to be buttoned and the lapels are short; the faux three-button, which is nothing but a two-button jacket with an extra, topmost idle button and buttonhole; and a "2½" or "roll through," on which the top button is idle, but the lapel roll is gradual so that its line is longer than a true three-button but shorter than a two-button. And I say that true three-button jackets look bad on everyone, because a jacket's waist button is meant to be a fulcrum that allows its top and bottom to expand and contract as you move, but closing that third button freezes the chest in place, causing the shoulders and back to pull, and making you look stiff. Nor can you leave the top button undone, because the jacket's front will still look closed and you boxy. Nonetheless, true three-buttons worn this way harm the diminutive man the least. Faux three-buttons, favored by old-money Americans, harm no one. The roll-through, favored by the Italians, benefits everyone, especially the diminutive, for its lapels tend to be narrower, and the idle button and buttonhole, though never closed, add slightly to the illusion of height because the additional button tricks the eye into believing the jacket is longer.

And, as is the common understanding, the diminutive man should not wear double-breasted jackets. Their extra flap of cloth in front increases his sense of bulk; their double set of buttons increases his sense of width; and their peaked lapels, which come to a point above the bottom of the collar, add an unhelpful pair of near-horizontal lines. The net effect is to make him look like a fireplug, and men who look like fireplugs look ridiculous. Yet in spite of these dangers, many diminutive men nonetheless insist on wearing them.

And truly it is a very natural and ordinary thing to desire to be well attired, and always, when men wear stylish garments who can, they will be praised or not blamed; but when they cannot, and wear them anyway, here lie the error and the blame. Thus the diminutive man who is drawn to double-breasted jackets should consider instead single-breasted jackets with peaked lapels—the model Bogart wore the day after Miles Archer was shot. Despite the absence of this garment from department stores and the scorn of the designer Hardy Amies, it is nonetheless proper—and, because of its smartness and its rarity, is greatly favored by dandies. And if someone should say: but peaked lapels add to the horizontal line, I reply with the reasons given above: that it is the double row of buttons and extra cloth of double-breasted jackets that create the added sense of width and make peaked lapels look like the arms of a fire hydrant, whereas on single-breasted suits they look rakish. And if some others should suggest that diminutive men who want to wear double-breasted suits ought to wear them with notched lapels, I reply with what I will say below on double-breasted garments and how they should be employed. From this one may draw a general rule that never or rarely fails: whoever wears that which accentuates the way his body is, at the expense of how it should appear, is ruined.

IV.

Why the Double-Breasted Suits Which Humphrey Bogart Wore Did Not Look Ridiculous on Humphrey Bogart's Frame

The difficulties arising from diminutive men wearing double-breasted suits having been considered, one might marvel at how it happened that Humphrey Bogart, a diminutive man, wore double-breasted suits and nonetheless did not look ridiculous. I reply that all double-breasted suits of which memory remains have been one of two diverse kinds: either they have had peaked lapels, side or no vents, and six buttons arranged in three vertically equidistant pairs with the top pair being half again as far apart as the bottom two, and with functioning button-holes for both the middle and lower-right buttons; or they deviate from the above.

In recent times the examples of these two diverse kinds were seen on David Letterman and the late Johnnie Cochran. For years, Letterman wore nothing but double-breasted suits of the utmost rakishness and propriety. Their chief virtue is the jackets' button stance, which forms as it were a double-legged martini glass that buttons at the middle row, or something like the illustration below:

```
    •        •

       •  •

       •  •
```

Tailors call this a "six-on-two" (sometimes shortened to "6 × 2") jacket, since there are six total buttons, two of which can be buttoned, the other four being for show. But Johnnie Cochran's suits were examples of the most common and vulgar deviation from the classic mode: their button stance forms a keystone that buttons only at the bottom row:

```
    •        •

       •  •

       •  •
```

This is called a "six-on-one." And though the trapezoid is not a flattering shape on a man's body, these suits are seen and sold everywhere. Thus whoever considers the one and the other will find in some respects more difficulty in acquiring the mode of Letterman, but should it be found, great panache in wearing it. So inversely, you will find ease in acquiring the mode of Cochran, but great unsightliness in wearing it.

The causes of the difficulty of being able to acquire the mode of Letterman are that it is more difficult to tailor, and thus no longer favored by the industry, and that American tastes have declined, as will be discussed. Yet this mode is more versatile; for, depending on how the lapels are rolled, it can be buttoned at the middle button, which effects an authoritative, serious look, or at the bottom button, effecting a casual, relaxed look. But suits like Cochran's are a corruption of the "Kent" model, invented by the duke of Windsor's third brother to flatter the diminutive physique. This has four buttons and a long lapel roll, but also a high buttoning point, whereas the other mode buttons far below the waist and looks out of balance.

However many its buttons, a double-breasted jacket will always have peaked lapels, for notched lapels on them are an abomination. Aside from being ahistorical (for the double-breasted suit is the direct descendent of the frock coat, the business and formal coat of the 19th century, which always took peaked lapels) and a sartorial oxymoron (for the more formal ought not be coupled with the less within the same garment), they destroy the suggestion of broad shoulders and a chiseled physique that peaked lapels help create. To see this, one has only to consider the double-breasted suits of Alex Trebek, host of *Jeopardy*, who—unlike many far-better-dressed men—earns more than enough to afford the best custom tailors but nonetheless acquires his clothes through a promotional deal with a third-rate manufacturer. The peaked lapels should each always carry a buttonhole, always angle upward, and always come to a sharp point. Some designers and tailors leave a space (visible on the suits of CBS News correspondent Ed Bradley) to effect an antique and slightly more casual look; lapels cut flush against the collar are sharper and more precise. Once such a suit has been found, tried on, and judged satisfactory, one has only to fear a center vent. If this is eliminated— that is, sewn shut by a competent tailor—there remains nothing else to fear from the suit, provided it is of a suitable cloth, as will be discussed.

The contrary occurs with suits like Cochran's. Buttons that are arranged like a keystone destroy the noble lies effected by a double-breasted jacket's shape because instead of effecting straight lines at the abdomen—which make one look more substantial—they effect unflattering diagonal lines which make the waist seem lower, the abdomen both longer and wider, and the legs shorter, illusions from which no man benefits. For the reasons given, they can open the way for you to be mistaken for a Garment District huckster. Nor is it enough for you to eliminate a center vent or effect any other positive changes, because it is the button stance and cut that are the true defects, and these cannot be changed.

Now if you consider the nature of Bogart's double-breasted suits, you will find them similar to those of Letterman. Therefore, since Bogart chose the proper mode instead of the vulgar, and because he often wore them buttoned at the bottom button, effecting a long lapel roll (and thus a longer vertical line), his diminutive stature did not hamper his looking smart. But his tailor added another touch: he set the buttons higher and also closer together, narrowing what tailors call the "crossover" or "wrap" to five inches or even less. This sharpens the angle of the peaked lapels, thus further emphasizing the vertical line. These innovations made Bogart seem both less wide and more tall, without effecting the harmful illusions discussed above. Having considered all these things, therefore, no one will marvel at the stylishness which Bogart and Aristotle Onassis, and in our time the television host Tony Brown, exhibit in their double-breasted suits, nor at the difficulties others such as James Cagney and Harry Truman had in looking smart in theirs. This has come both from the disparity of their suits and also the virtue and prudence of the wearers.

V.

Of Tall Men

But, coming to those so tall that double-breasted suits never harm them but always help, their needs are the opposite of those discussed above. For tall men tend to look gawky, gangly, or gaunt—rather like Ichabod Crane. Heavier cloths, such as flannels and tweeds, and also busier patterns, such as plaids and windowpanes, make him look more substantial and less like a beanpole. And in the case of shirtings, checks are most efficacious; in neckwear stripes; and in accessories boldness and clutter: the tall man's breast pocket should always house a handkerchief; his shirts should take cufflinks; his tie can be bold and should always be clipped; his shirt collars look good pinned. Stripes, whether on suits or shirts, do not help the tall man, and cause great harm if they are narrow and close together. And he ought to avoid bow ties, especially with suits and always in the absence of a vest.

The tall man should never wear skimpy or tight-fitting clothes, for they only make him look leaner and thus taller, as do jackets with square, built-up shoulders or narrow lapels, or that have no vents, or that do not cover his seat; and nothing contributes more to a tall man's ruin than a short jacket. If he can find a jacket with shoulders that extend slightly beyond his natural width, so much the better; but he must take care that they are not so broad as to suggest NFL equipment, nor so stiff as to be uncomfortable or restrictive of movement. His lapel notches should fall slightly below the collarbone; any higher will make his jacket look too small. And the jacket's outer hip pockets should be even with the bottom buttonhole or slightly above, to compress the vertical line.

And, as was said, double-breasted jackets are most useful for the tall, because their double row of buttons and extra flap of cloth add to the sense of width at the expense of height, and also because all those buttons and flaps and peaked lapels augment that clutter praised above. But he should never button them at the bottom button but always at the waist, for the long lapel roll effects height that he does not need.

In terms of detail, the more the better. Thus the tall man's jacket should always have four outside pockets, and except for the breast pocket, these should always have flaps. Most jackets seen in America will only have three pockets—one over the left breast, and one over each hip. Custom tailors will add a fourth, called a "ticket" or "cash" pocket by the English (for some say that they were first added to accommodate railway tickets, others to carry money for tipping gatekeepers while on the hunt), that sits just above the right hip pocket and is about half its size. Purists will say that ticket pockets are a sporting detail that have no place on town suitings; but dandies like them for the extra panache they impart. On trousers, cuffs are essential—at least an inch and three-quarters; an inch and seven-eighths for the very tall—as are pleats, because their extra fullness adds bulk.

With respect to shirtings, he should ensure that his wardrobe includes many checks, small plaids, and busy antique and even horizontal stripes. Assuming that like most tall men his neck is long, he must also ensure that his collars sit higher—as much as a half inch higher—than is standard on ready-made shirts, lest all that protruding neck make him look like a stork. And he must take care that his collars are not too small for his frame, but such considerations are treated at length in their place. Boldly patterned and brightly colored ties work better for him than for other men, although striped ties, because they break up verticality, benefit most.

I wish the example of talk show host Conan O'Brien to suffice. Architecturally, his clothes are sound. But in no other respect do they benefit his lofty frame. And this is doubtless owing to the influence of some media image consultant or network wardrobe prince who professes knowledge of what ought to be worn on television. And truly if his client were a politician or some other burdened by the necessity that he offend no one, the advice would be sound. But in the case of a show-business personality it is harmful, for people expect those with more money, more fame, and more delightful jobs than themselves to be more stylish; and when they are not, they do not respect them, for they consider that so much opportunity to cut loose has been squandered.

In all Conan makes these five errors: he does not wear patterns; always wears dark worsteds; never wears a handkerchief nor any other detail or accessory; rarely wears striped ties; does not wear double-breasted jackets. Yet these errors would not hurt him if he did not make a sixth: wearing true three-button single-breasted jackets. For these jackets are most deleterious to the tall man, because their high closure and narrow lapels create a vast expanse of cloth across the chest that covers so much shirt and tie which, when exposed, help to break up verticality. And if someone should suggest that he wear his jacket unbuttoned, I reply that nothing is more sloppy, especially for the tall man, for his jacket being of necessity longer, there is more of it flapping about and drawing attention away from his face. And so a prudent tall man will eschew these errors, and attire himself more in the mode of Fox anchor Brit Hume, who adheres to the rules set forth above.

VI.

Of Those Whose Bodies Look Good
Thanks to Fortune

No one should marvel if, in speaking of slender men and how they ought to dress, I bring up the greatest examples. For in every era there is an ideal body shape, and that era's clothing is always geared toward it. In the Renaissance men wore doublets and tunics that complemented the short and stocky build favored in those times. In the 18th and early 19th centuries, when so much time on horseback developed men's calf and thigh muscles, they wore tight breeches and hose to "show a fine leg," as the saying went. In the late 19th century, after industrialization created so many new millionaires, fatness became prized as a sign of prosperity, and dark vested suits with long coats became the norm. Since the slender build has been our most admired form for well nigh a century, it should not be surprising that our era's clothes are designed to flatter it, nor that the greatest dressers of our time were so formed. And since men almost always walk on paths beaten by others and proceed in their dress by imitation, a prudent man should always enter upon the paths beaten by great dressers, and imitate those who have been most excellent, so that if his own virtue does not reach that far, it is at least in the odor of it. He should do as prudent marksmen do when the place they plan to hit appears too distant, and knowing how far the strength of their rifle carries, they set their aim much higher than the place intended, not to reach such a height with their bullet, but to be able with the aid of so high an aim to achieve their design.

I say, then, that slender men, being favored by fortune both for the reasons given above and because their form is especially flattered by the most stylish fabrics, patterns, and details, have had among their ranks more dressers of consummate virtue than men of any other build. And because an affinity for fine clothes is easily discouraged or never takes root in those to whom it appears that clothes will never look good on them, we should wonder even less that in our era slender men have all but monopolized the roster of outstanding dandies. But to come to those who have shown the greatest virtue in things sartorial, I say that the most excellent are Anthony Eden, Fred Astaire, the duke of Windsor, Cary Grant, and the like. And although one should not dwell too much on Eden, as he was an elected politician and so most of the time was forced to wear dark worsteds, nonetheless he should be admired if only for that virtue which enabled him to recognize and exploit every opportunity he had to make a profession of style within the strictures placed upon him, such as having his single-breasted suits made with peaked lapels. But let us consider Astaire and the others who have dressed with consummate style; and if their particular habits are examined, one sees that they availed themselves of every stylish mode available, and even created some new ones.

The duke, in concert with his tailor, devised the single greatest mode for tailored clothing of the last century, discussed at length below; brought suede shoes and plaid suits to town; wore the first evening shirt with a turn-down collar; invented the cutaway collar to accommodate the large tie knots he favored; had a hand in the invention of many other new modes; and revived many under-used yet elegant old modes. Astaire, by wearing clothes that were at once stylish and comfortable, was first to show the stuffed shirts in their boiled collars and stiff coats how little is to be esteemed whoever dresses as they do; is said to have invented the "puff" mode of folding pocket handkerchiefs; and more than anyone else showed the infinite possibilities afforded by taking due account of one's socks. Grant made solid ties chic; and, indeed, with his gray suits, white shirts, and silver ties, he invented the "monochromatic" look before Regis Philbin learned to tie a tie. These innovations made good dressers great, and their excellent virtue enabled them to devise modes that advanced the cause of style and redound to their eternal glory.

Those whose slender forms are similarly favored by our era's clothing may not indeed be innovators of such rank, but they may benefit from those good innovations conceived by others, and also from all the other elements of stylish dress mentioned above and discussed below. And the slender man ought to know that the slightness of his form looks best when beefed up by flannels,

tweeds, and twills (cloth with parallel diagonal ribs), and spread
out by plaids, windowpanes, and checks; when it is draped in easy
fitting, natural-shouldered jackets and pleated, full-cut trousers;
and when it is accessorized with cufflinks, pocket handkerchiefs,
and tie clasps. And since all of these are more stylish than their
plainer cousins or their lack, truly the slender man is more blessed
by fortune than any other. Eden, Astaire, Grant, and Windsor
would not have achieved the heights they did had they not been
able to wear all of these modes.

To such high examples I want to adduce a lesser example, but it
will have some proportion with the others and I want it to suffice
for all other similar cases: this is Adolphe Menjou. From humble
beginnings he became a prince of Hollywood. Nor did he receive
anything from fortune other than the opportunity. And at a time
when all Hollywood was coming under the yoke of costume designers, he steadfastly refused to change his personal style but—
like the others mentioned above—always wore his own custom
suits, shoes, and shirts. And he was of such virtue that, recognizing his opportunities, he let none of them pass but always attired
himself with great panache and consummate style.

VII.

Of Those Whose Bodies Look Good
Owing to Virtue

Those with a chiseled, muscular physique—almost always the product more of their own virtue than of fortune—attract attention with little trouble but attire themselves with much. For what makes their physique so striking also makes it difficult to clothe. For most men the difference between their chest and waist measurements (called the "drop") is rarely greater than six inches, and most suits are made accordingly. But the muscular man's torso is usually much larger than his waist. For decades, no suits were made to accommodate this difference, and the muscular had to make do with trousers so ample that even when altered they did not fit properly, owing to that havoc that excessive alterations wreak on the silhouette of any garment. But in our time stores sell what the industry calls "athletic cut" suits, which pair large jackets with much smaller trousers. The muscular man who buys off-the-rack is forced to buy only this kind, for none but it has any chance of fitting him. His only alternative is to place himself in the hands of a custom tailor.

To both modes of attiring the muscular, I want to adduce two examples that have occurred within our memory; and these are Dan Dierdorf and Arnold Schwarzenegger. Dierdorf became a television commentator from football player, which necessitated a change of wardrobe; and even one lacking a trained eye can see that he has not made the transition well. On the other hand Schwarzenegger, called "Aah-nold" by the people, accomplished a more difficult transition with greater facility. And this arose not so much from his greater virtue, nor even his superior style, but from his astuteness in understanding that his frame is best served by custom tailoring. For no ready-made suit, not even those deemed "athletic cut," can handsomely clothe the muscular man, because even if the trousers are not too large, the jacket will be, for all ready-made jackets are sized according to their circumference at the chest, and where this is large, the rest will be large; for large ready-made jackets are not made for the muscular but for the rotund, as the industry calculates that what is large can be reduced to fit the smaller but what is small cannot be made larger. This is ruinous to the muscular, because a jacket that fits at the top will be much too big in the middle and bottom; and it cannot be altered to your satisfaction, because extensive changes ruin its silhouette. For this must be realized: the very term "athletic cut" is a fraud, for such suits are not cut differently at all, but merely paired differently, as was said.

But custom tailoring is expensive, and Arnold is rich; so the muscular man of limited means might despair that he has no remedy at all. But he can have his suits "made-to-measure," a middle way between true custom tailoring (called "bespoke" by the English, for the garment is held not to exist, even in the abstract, until the customer "bespeaks" it) and buying off-the-rack. This allows the muscular man to order a suit whose jacket fits him in the chest and shoulders and is not billowy through the waist and hips; and whose trousers fit him in the waist but whose legs are not reminiscent of harem pants. And the cost of made-to-measure, though more than off-the-rack, is less than bespoke, so you can afford it.

Coming to the modes in which muscular men should dress, they need jackets with unpadded (or lightly padded) shoulders, for what all that padding is meant to provide they already possess; and its addition to their substantial form is worse than redundant. They should avoid jackets with very nipped waists, as these only accentuate the chest. Nonetheless, since straight-hanging jackets make them look fat by effecting a waist every bit as large as their massive chest, they should choose jackets with at least a hint of waist suppression. They must also avoid jackets with narrow lapels, as these will be overwhelmed by their chest, making them look over-wide. They should always wear trousers that sit on the natural waist, for these both lengthen their legs and balance the appearance of their hips with respect to their barrel torsos. And they should avoid tiny shirt collars and dainty shoes, lest they be derided as girly men.

But to come to those modes that help them, smooth worsteds—solid, striped, or of some elongating pattern—are most beneficial, as are striped shirts with long point collars. Ventless, two-button, single-breasted jackets also help. Whereas double-breasted jackets hurt them for the same reason they help the tall and slender; and three-button ones, especially when buttoned at the top, ruin you by making you look like a fireplug, the quality of which was given above. Still worse is the "NBA-style" of four- or five- or even six-button jackets that close all the way up to the clavicle and hang almost to the knee. And the bigger and taller you are, the more you end up looking like an industrial smokestack.

So whoever compares Dierdorf, who wears ready-made "athletic cut" clothes acquired through a promotional deal with a retailer, to Schwarzenegger, who spends his own money on bespoke tailoring, will see how wide a disproportion there can be in the appearances of two men with similar physiques, all because of their varying modes of dress. For in addition to that error just mentioned, and also his insistence on lapels so narrow as to be invisible, Dierdorf worsens things by adhering to none of the other modes set forth above save one: for in always wearing a blazer, he is always wearing dark worsteds. But he could learn from Schwarzenegger that ubiquity is not necessary, and that so long as the architecture of your clothes is sound, many modes remain for you to risk a profession of style.

VIII.

How Men of Superfluous Girth
May Minimize Their Appearance

When those bodies that are to be adorned are more ample than is the norm, there are three modes by which one may minimize their appearance: first, diet them; second, exercise them; third, dress them in dark, easy-fitting, solid or striped, ventless, two-button single-breasted suits. For since these draw attention neither to horizontal lines nor to one's bulk, and also lie smoothly on one's form, they avoid effecting the "stuffed sausage" look—the error described by Wodehouse when he wrote that one of his characters "looked as if he had been poured into his clothes and forgot to say 'when!'"

The modes that help the heavy are mostly the same as those that benefit the diminutive, for that which emphasizes height also deëmphasizes bulk. And the only exceptions are shirt collars and waists. Long, angular collars countervail soft, round faces. And whereas a nipped waist is beneficial to most men, it is a curse to the heavy. For most men's shoulders are wider than their middle, and when their jacket's waist is narrower than its shoulders, this enhances the noble lies discussed at length above. But the opposite is true for the heavy man, for whom a jacket waist narrower than its shoulders only calls attention to bulk; for since his actual waist is bigger, not smaller, than his shoulders, a jacket with a narrow waist must of necessity pull, pinch and gape around his middle. And since nothing is more ruinous to his appearance than this, great care must be taken so that not just the jacket's waist but every aspect of every garment is cut generously enough to fall smoothly with no visible furrows or pulls, and without coming to rest on his belly, hips, or behind, like so much cloth draped over a shelf. The exception might be if the jacket's shoulders could be built out enough to balance its hips yet without overwhelming his head or causing the upper sleeves to collapse inward; then a touch of waist suppression would improve his proportions. Three-button jackets should be avoided, especially those that button at the top, for these will make him look upholstered. Trousers should be worn at the natural waist, both to cover the belly and lengthen the leg line, and they should have "forward" or "English" pleats: two each on each side of the fly, facing inward. These best hide bulk, especially when viewed from the side, by which vantage the belly is most prominent, and also allow the trouser legs to fall straight down from the waistband; whereas narrow trouser legs call attention to the great mass sitting atop them, making him look like Humpty Dumpty.

Whether double-breasted jackets help or harm the heavy man, no two writers can be found who agree. For some say that they should never be worn, others that they should be worn only in certain modes, and still others that they are a godsend in any mode. I believe that, on the whole, they should be avoided because their clutter and button stance emphasize width at the expense of height. And if someone should say: so long as the lapels are rolled to the bottom button, they are good, because the long lapel roll accentuates height, I reply that the illusion of width caused by their peaked lapels and double row of buttons fights against this. And if still others should argue that their extra flap of cloth covers his paunch, I respond that this is better accomplished with a single-breasted vest, worn with the jacket unbuttoned, as this presents three long vertical lines where he needs them most.

As examples there are Sydney Greenstreet and Babe Ruth. Sydney Greenstreet dressed in drapey, mostly chalk-striped, three-piece, single-breasted suits, yet he looked fat. Babe Ruth, in order to get in shape for an upcoming baseball season, sometimes exercised vigorously, and at the start of a few seasons did not look so fat. Later in life he wanted to look slimmer much as Sydney Greenstreet had, by dressing in loose-fitting, striped garments. But he did not succeed, and looked corpulent until an accident caused him to lose a great deal of weight. For in truth there is no secure mode of minimizing one's appearance other than to employ a judicious combination of the first two mentioned above. And whoever finds himself succumbing to gluttony and indolence and does not minimize them, should expect to be maximized by them; for these will always increase if they are not suppressed at every turn, and their increase will always spell the increase of your form. But when bodies are used to being large and there is little prospect that they will ever be otherwise, then it is indeed useful to dress them in the manner described above.

Here we may learn from the ladies, who so often wear dark solids because they know that while these may not make them look thin, they do avoid making them look any fatter—something many other modes assuredly do, especially bold patterns, bright colors, and bulky cloths. And done well these modes may actually make the stout man look a bit smaller, as Tom Wolfe writes of one of his characters: "His smooth jowls welled up from out of a white shirt of lustrous Sea Island cotton. A beautifully made gray worsted suit lay upon every square inch of his buttery body without a ripple. He wore a solid navy tie and a pair of black shoes so well cut they made his feet look tiny. He was sleek as a beaver." Anyone who doubts this is possible should watch Jackie Gleason in *The Hustler*. He wore his own three-piece bespoke suit and made all his own shots, never taking off his jacket, causing Eddie Felson to marvel at his elegance and agility. And careful attention to his clothes allowed him to defeat a much younger rival despite drinking a whole bottle of whiskey and playing pool for forty straight hours. But it is much more difficult to make an ample body look slimmer than a slim one stouter, so that the only secure path is to diet them and exercise them.

IX.

Of Those Who Suffer
from Irregularities

But because one encounters particularities of body which cannot be altogether attributed either to stature or to girth, I do not think they should be left out. These are sloping or square shoulders, bow legs or knock-knees, stooping or swayed-back posture, and any number of imbalances that can occur in body parts that come in pairs. And truly men who suffer from deformities of this kind suffer from a further disadvantage: they cannot be accommodated by ready-made clothing because it will never fit their form, no matter how extensively it is altered. Indeed the more it is altered the worse it will look, as its original form is increasingly ruined. And still worse, these men cannot be accommodated with made-to-measure because their deformities are too grave for the minor adjustments possible with such clothing.

Nonetheless, clothing can disguise and even hide all of the above afflictions, provided it is made for you by a tailor who knows what he is doing. For this must be understood: whereas made-to-measure garments are cut from existing patterns that have been modified slightly, bespoke garments are cut from patterns that have been drafted from scratch according to the dimensions of the particular client. In addition, made-to-measure clothes are manufactured in far-off places, eliminating the chance for more than one fitting, and by tailors who have neither measured nor even seen you; but bespoke garments are cut, fitted, and finished in the same shop, so that you may try on the clothes at each stage of their construction, and by the same tailor who measures you and draws your pattern, offering him infinite chances to correct and adjust the fit. These modes allow bespoke tailors to construct garments to suit any man's needs, be he very tall or very short, very thin or very fat, very muscular or very gaunt; and it allows them to hide or mitigate almost any deformity. I wish to demonstrate this with two examples, one classic, the other modern; and I judge it sufficient, for whoever would find it necessary, to imitate them.

Cary Grant's head was overlarge in proportion to his body, but this is not noticeable when you see him in films, nor did he ever look ungainly because of it. This arose from nothing other than his wisdom in understanding that this defect was easily concealed by jackets with slightly wider shoulders. And since the rest of him was not afflicted by any defect, the remainder of his suits could be cut normally; whereas had he bought a suit with bigger shoulders ready-made, not only would the shoulders not have fit him (for on his bespoke suits, only the top shoulderline was longer, but under the arms and around his chest the suits fit normally), but the rest of the suit would have been baggy.

In our time, Tony Blair, Prime Minister of the United Kingdom, suffers from a stooped posture. And though this is noticeable when one looks at him, its awkwardness is minimized by the virtue of his tailor, for if he wore off-the-peg suits, you would notice a great swath of cloth bunching up around the back of his neck. But tailors know how to correct this, so that even though that stoop is still visible, at least his jackets fit and their back is smooth.

Infinite other examples could be adduced to demonstrate the virtues of bespoke tailoring. But those fortunate enough to suffer from no deformities whatsoever, and to fall perfectly within one of the industry's arbitrary sizing categories, do not need to incur the time and expense of bespoke, and may be satisfied by off-the-rack clothing.

X.

In What Mode
All Well-Dressed Men
Should Be Measured

In examining the qualities of these body types, one must admit another consideration; that is whether, whatever his shape, a man's clothes fit adequately or if he is always under the necessity of pulling here and adjusting there so that they are not perpetually in discord with his frame. And, to better clarify this issue, I judge those to be attired in well-fitting clothes who, when they are standing, their jackets' collars sit flush against the back of their necks and collarbones and allow a half inch of shirt collar to show above; whose lapels descend unbent and unbuckled down his chest; whose sleeves extend exactly to the wristbone of each arm and no farther, and whose shirt sleeves extend to the base of each palm, so that a half-inch of linen is always exposed (give or take an eighth depending on his height); whose jackets are long enough to cover their seat, and nowhere bunch, pull, or crease, nor appear to be slipping off their shoulders, nor do the vents gape to expose shirt cloth or waistband but remain closed; and whose trousers do not pull around the abdomen, nor do any pockets or pleats open, nor does either leg expose any sock, but is barely long enough to rest on top of each shoe. These are but the minimum requirements of fit, discernible by anyone and necessary for everyone. I implore all men to learn and retain them and not to rely on salesmen to tell you if a garment fits, for salesmen are untrustworthy, as will be discussed.

The clothes of talk show host Jay Leno are correct in all of the above respects, exhibit no defects, and never require adjustment while he is wearing them, because they fit so well that no amount of gesticulation can disorient them; though among the other things he should have learned from Carson is always to show some linen. Or if you prefer films, rent *Rope;* the clothes of the two murderers and their accomplice Jimmy Stewart fit as well as any garments ever have. All of these good effects derive from the virtue of their tailors, men with knowledge of how clothes must fit and the skill to assure that they do. Not all tailors have both, and some have neither, especially those employed by department stores. But the best bespoke tailors understand and can accommodate the most arcane aspects of fit, which are too complex and subtle to be discussed here. By contrast, the suits you will find in department stores, even if altered by the most virtuous tailor, will never fit as well as one that is bespoke. This arises from their being made to fit anyone, for garments made to fit anyone end up fitting no one. In clothing as in architecture, proportion and harmony are paramount, and these are offended by ill-fitting clothes. But well-fitting clothes would please even Ictinus and Callicrates and will always be a credit to their wearer.

XI.

Of the Young Man

It remains now only to reason about young men. All difficulties regarding them come from others' perceptions. These alone have bodies and cannot adorn them; they have pleasing shapes, and cannot profit from them; they arouse expectations because of their youth, causing anger when it is perceived that they are not attired correctly; and when well attired, arousing resentment. Thus only these men are subject to rules not based on reasoned aesthetics. But as they are not a specific body type but can be any of those discussed above, I will omit speaking of them. Nonetheless, if someone were to inquire of me how it comes about that they arouse this hatred even though those whom they upset are so much more eminent—and yet can be driven to fits of apoplexy by the attire of someone half their age—though this is known, it does not seem superfluous to me to recall a good part of it to memory.

And I say that the cause is envy. For it is very ordinary and reasonable that the old should envy the young, to whom it is given to enjoy so many more pleasures, so much more intensely, for so much longer. Truly, we would marvel if they did not envy them. And this envy extends to dress, because old men wish to reserve to themselves the few pleasures which remain to them to enjoy. Thus they get angry when they see young men wearing double-breasted suits and French cuff shirts. It does not seem reasonable to them that young men should enjoy the trappings of eminence before attaining the reality. Michael Lewis writes in his book *Liar's Poker* of being warned by an older colleague not to wear suspenders to Wall Street because these were considered reserved for men above a certain rank.

So the young must take great care not to offend with fanciness. This is difficult for them, for by nature they prefer the loud and garish, thinking that these will help them rise above the multitude, or will best attract girls. And while ostentation can indeed make them notorious, rare is the young swell who survives into middle age with his reputation unsullied. Benjamin Disraeli made himself famous through his clothes; yet when he wanted to enter politics, he knew that he had to give up red shoes and purple trousers and yellow waistcoats. And these excesses of his youth delayed his rise, for he did not become prime minister until age 64 (dressed head-to-toe in black). Had he been more prudent as a young man, he might have beaten the record set by the younger Pitt. The safer course is to dress plainly when young, and then cut loose once you are older or have attained so much reputation that none but the most insolent would dare rebuke you. Tom Wolfe did not start wearing white suits until he had three best-sellers to his name; after that, he could have worn tri-cornered hats without harm.

In addition to those modes mentioned above, these especially are to be avoided by the young man: three-piece suits (especially if the vest is double-breasted), contrast-collar shirts, two-tone or crocodile or anything but solid calf shoes, hats, pocket watches, bow ties, handkerchiefs, bold patterns and bright colors. And these work well for them: blazers and khakis, single-breasted suits, plain black shoes, shirts with barrel cuffs and button down collars, striped ties, belts, subtle patterns and somber colors. And if someone should complain that these rules leave him no room within which to make a profession of style but consign him to dreariness, I reply that necessity forces them on him.

Although the dress of television pundit Tucker Carlson is not particularly fancy or even smart, he nonetheless dresses in a manner that would infuriate older colleagues were they not already infuriated by his preternatural success. And specifically I mean his ubiquitous bow ties. These have the desired effect of making him stand out, but at the cost of making him look pretentious. For it never or rarely happens that you see him on television and someone with you does not say, "Who does he think he is with that bow tie? George Will?"

So the young man must avoid these modes lest he provoke the same response, and his career is ruined. And the young man should observe the correct modes above all when he interviews for jobs. There dandification most harms him, because it is much easier not to hire someone than to fire him, and those who are held pretentious or insolent will not be hired. So when interviewing, he should attire himself in the modes recommended above; and once the job is his, attire himself according to those modes common in his office, taking care not to out-dress the boss (unless the latter dresses so badly that there is no choice), but going as far as he can in the direction of elegance without giving offense. And if he does this well, someone may say of him, as the business writers might have said of the young Jack Welch, that "he lacks nothing of being a CEO except a corner office." Thus can clothes help one gain employment and prevent one from losing it.

XII.

How Many Kinds of
Silhouettes There Are and
Concerning Designer Suits

H aving discoursed in particular on all the qualities of those body types which at the beginning I proposed to reason about, having considered in some part the causes of their looking smart or shoddy, and having shown the modes in which one may improve their appearance, it remains for me now to discourse generally on the various silhouettes in which garments are made. We have said above that it is necessary for a man to present a pleasing shape; otherwise his appearance must of necessity be ruined. The principal factors that determine the appearance of every man's shape, slender ones as well as muscular or fat, are his actual shape and his clothes' silhouette. And because there cannot be a pleasing shape without a good silhouette, and where there is a good silhouette there is always a pleasing shape, I shall leave off reasoning on shape and shall speak of silhouette.

I say, therefore, that silhouette—also called "cut," because its effects are achieved primarily through the pattern according to which the cloth of a garment is cut—is both the general outline of a garment and also the particular qualities that constitute it, as when tailors speak of the "cut" of a jacket's shoulders. Silhouette is often confused with fit, but this is an error, for all garments must fit the same way in certain respects no matter their silhouette, as was said. Besides, as a very astute commentator has written, "the concept of fit is somewhat nonsensical." No sensible man wants his clothes to conform exactly to the shape of his body; for this, as has been discussed at length, may or may not be pleasing. The virtue of tailored clothing is that it improves a man's rudimentary shape. And it is truer than any other truth that where the appearance of a man's shape is not pleasing to the eye, no matter what its rudimentary shape, it is the fault of his clothes' silhouette. Saul Bellow tells us that the philosopher Allan Bloom's love of beautiful and useless things extended to fine clothes; and he indicates Bloom's understanding of silhouette when he makes him say of Bellow's Chicago tailor that "he makes mafiosi-type clothes, not for the dons but for the soldiers." For since one can order even the plainest cloth—and not just electric blue gangster stripes—from any tailor, this means nothing other than that this tailor's cut was so garish that the godfathers, who adhered to the Wall Street adage that one should "dress British, think Yiddish," would not wear it even in plain gray worsted.

In general, garments may sit close to the body, projecting a slender shape; or they may hang loosely, effecting a wider look.

They may elongate your form or shorten it. They may effect severe angles or soft, gentle curves. And they may be structured and built up, which gives a military impression, or else very soft, which makes them appear nonchalant and comfortable. Structure and softness are determined largely by the type of materials used: a structured jacket will have more padding in the shoulders, and stiffer canvas in the chest. The other qualities that constitute silhouette are determined by the cut. And because these can be combined to form an infinite number of shapes, truly it may be said that there are as many silhouettes as there are suits, or at any rate manufacturers and tailors. But the elements that make them up are the same, and these you must understand.

Beginning at the top, I say that a jacket's shoulders are its most important parts because, being so close to your face, they dominate your appearance, and also because the rest of your jacket literally hangs therefrom. The first consideration is width: shoulders may end exactly at your deltoid, or else extend by a half inch or so. Second, a shoulderline may be straight and square; it may be concave, curving downward from the collar and then rising toward the outer edge (called a "pitched" or "pagoda" shoulder); or it may slope downward or even be slightly convex. The third consideration is padding. Squared or pitched or raised or sculpted shoulders need padding to achieve their look. Sloped shoulders take very thin, soft padding, and little of it, effecting a casual, almost natural look. And since there is confusion regarding the meaning of "natural shoulder," I want to discourse on it briefly. The term is sometimes used to mean a shoulder that is no wider than your body's shoulder, sometimes to indicate one that is sloped like the natural shoulderline, sometimes to refer to one with no padding, and sometimes to some combination of these. And truly, the most natural of shoulders would be one that partook in all three qualities. But padding and line are the most important, and many a natural shoulder is slightly extended yet so soft that the sleevehead (where the shoulder meets the upper sleeve) gently cascades over the deltoid. Some tailors believe that this rounded effect looks more natural than a precisely fitted shoulderline. Beyond this, a shoulder may also be smooth or "roped" (or as the Italians say, *"con rollino"*); that is, the sleevehead may be raised up a quarter-inch or so above the shoulderline. And, viewed from the side, a sleevehead may be circular or else effect a more oval shape.

Descending next to armholes, called "scyes" by tailors, the generality of men are used to them being large since on most ready-made jackets they are enormous—"as big as the Holland Tunnel"—and men believe these to be more comfortable. Nonetheless, the best-dressed men have always preferred small, high armholes, because these allow greater freedom of movement and do not cause the rest of your jacket to leap off your body when you move your arms.

Moving to the front, the "gorge" is where the lapels and collar meet; the line that separates them is called the "gorge line." This may be high—at the collarbone or slightly above—or lower, in the upper ribcage. Lapels are the most elegantly useless part of a jacket. Originally they served to cover the chest in harsh weather—hence the buttonhole on the left lapel, which fastened to a button underneath the right—yet when folded back they allowed for greater airiness in warmth. In our time they are purely decorative. Well-styled lapels extend at their widest point about halfway across the chest. Savile Row tailors tend to cut them slightly narrower, the Neapolitans a touch wider. Their edges may be straight, convex—effecting what tailors call "belly"—or even slightly concave. Lapels may also be peaked or else slope down from the collar, effecting a "notch." Notched lapels may be greatly sloped, culminating in the very wide gap favored by designers, or else have a very narrow gap, effecting what the industry calls a "fishmouth." The lapels worn by O. J. Simpson during his famous year-long television appearance, which had no gap at all, took a sound principle much too far. These extremes should be avoided in favor of moderate notches that sit high and whose openings point straight outward or even slightly up; downward-angled notches look sad and droopy. Above all, you should avoid notches that fall too low, as this makes the jacket look like the kind of thing rock musicians wore in the 1980s, with the sleeves bunched up around their elbows.

The chest of a jacket may be "swelled" or "lean," and "draped" or "clean." The outer edges of a lean chest lie fairly close to your torso. Those of a swelled chest billow out in a gentle curve from the armscye to the waist, making your chest look bigger. "Drape" is a slight excess of cloth in the hollow area of your chest below your collarbone, a fullness that manifests itself in subtle vertical ripples. Jackets that lie perfectly smooth are said to have a "clean chest."

Descending next to the waist, there are three considerations: if it exists, where it falls, and how dramatic it is. What the tailors call "waist suppression" is created by shaping the cloth with water and an iron, by the cut, by the front canvas, but mostly by darts. These last are created by cutting long slits on each side of the jacket, in the lower ribcage area, folding some cloth along each side of the slit into the jacket's innards, and then closing the hole with an inside stitch. Jackets with no darts generally have little or no waist, those with two darts a moderate waist, and those with four a pronounced waist. Waist suppression may be acute and angular, or rounded, like an hourglass; it may be short, coming to a sharp point, or long, gently tapering so that the narrow part continues for several inches; and its latitude may be at, higher, or lower than the wearer's natural waist. This is generally the narrowest diameter of a man's torso, unless he has a prominent belly, in which case it is the narrowest width of his torso, unless he is unusually corpulent; in all cases, it is the soft, fleshy area just below the ribcage and just above the hipbones.

The latitude of the coat's waist determines the placement of its buttons, called the "button stance." The "waist button" is the button that you actually fasten—the middle one on a three-button coat, or the top one on a two-button—and its placement is called the "buttoning point." One tailoring tradition holds that the waist button should fall a half inch below the wearer's natural waist. But the best dressed men know that a higher buttoning point is both slimming and elongating. A graceful buttoning point appears to bisect the jacket; but were it actually placed at the mathematical middle it would look too high. A general rule is to take half your jacket's length (measured from under the collar down the center back seam to the bottom edge), subtract perhaps an inch (give or take a fraction depending on your height), and then measure up from the jacket's front bottom edge. In all cases the waist button should be at or near the latitude of the jacket's waist, or narrowest point.

The "skirt" of a jacket is the portion that falls below the waist.

It may be very flared, emphasizing an angular look; hang straight, effecting what some call the "box" look; or else be fitted closely to the hip, actually curving inward slightly toward the bottom edge (which some tailors call "cupping"). On single-breasted jackets, the front edges below the waist button may hang straight or else form open quarters, as was said. On double-breasted jackets, only the edge of the outer flap is visible, and it should hang straight.

Descending then to trousers, truly their three most important qualities are "line, line, and line." Trousers that hang without buckles or ripples, especially along the creases, have good line. The half inch of additional length (called "break") favored by Americans is disdained by dandies because it disrupts this line. In addition, well-cut trousers follow the natural line of the body, fitting snuggly at the waist, filling out in the hips and upper thighs, and tapering gently down the rest of the leg to an opening that is two-thirds the size of the shoe. Straight or flared legs go in and out of fashion but never achieve the elegance of a well-tapered trouser. In general, such trousers will be roomy, and therefore comfortable, but you must take care not to let too much concern for comfort lead you to buy trousers that circus clowns might find useful. But coming to specifics, "rise" is the tailoring term for the distance from the crotch to the top of the waistband. As with arm-holes, the common opinion is that a longer rise makes for more comfortable trousers. While it is true that too short a rise is un-comfortable when standing and intolerable when sitting, too long a rise restricts the movement of the legs and also effects the "droopy-drawers" look. So your rise should be just long enough not to bind. All well-made trousers are higher in back than in the front, as this helps them accommodate the curve of your seat and remain in place. Trousers made by the English to be worn with suspenders will be dramatically higher in the back, with the waistband curving up to a fishmouth shape. Such trousers will always have forward pleats, whereas low-slung trousers worn at the hips can take outward-facing (or "reverse") pleats or even no pleats. Whether forward or reverse, the inner (or front) pleats should always be deeper than the outer (or back)—one to one and a half inches versus three-quarters of an inch or slightly less. And the fold of the inner pleats should lead directly to the trouser creases, which should always be centered, bisecting the knee. Flat-front trousers look best on those with no belly whatsoever, which helps to explain why they are so popular with the young. Yet pleats help maintain the trousers' line when you are standing and expand when you sit down, providing additional comfort. Thus to forgo them for the sake of fashion is not reasonable.

And the like can be said of infinite other aberrations. The most pernicious are extremely wide lapels, which make a man look like a gangster or a carnival barker; enormous shoulders, which make him look like a fashion illustration; and grossly exaggerated waist suppression, which makes him look like a woman. Any of these alone will provoke contempt and ridicule; together they ensure ruin.

And whoever considers the designer suits so popular in the 1970s and 1980s will find that, while in vogue for a brief time, they are today seen hardly at all, and only on those who do not mind being mistaken for talent agents or runway models. And by the end of that decade they had become so infamous that a popular novelist wrote a whole book to depict those who wore them as cannibals, drug addicts, and serial killers. The cause of their disappearance was their extreme styling, a defect of all designer suits in all times. For designer suits are useless and dangerous; and if one founds his wardrobe on them, he founds on mud, and will never be stylish or even safe. They are useless because they cannot be worn except during that moment when they are in fashion, which is fleeting; and even while it lasts, they are inferior to a well-styled garment. And they are dangerous because when worn they make their wearer look ridiculous and contemptible to those not enthralled by the same fashion; and when their moment has passed they take up precious closet space, taunting you and making you lament of money that should have been spent on something more longevous. For it does not matter how well made a garment is, or how luxurious its cloth, or how excellent it is in any other respect if its styling is ridiculous; whereas so long as a garment is handsomely styled, even if its quality is second-rate, it can be worn until it comes apart or the fabric becomes so shiny that women check their makeup by looking into your lapels.

I want to demonstrate better the failure of these suits. Designer silhouettes may be gargantuan or minimalist or both. If they are gargantuan, their sprawling lapels and shoulders reminiscent of football pads require shirts with collars as big as airplane wings and neckties as wide as scarves, neither of which are readily available in our time. And even if you can find them, wearing them will make you look like you stepped off the set of *Kojak*. The minimalist suits—those made with so little cloth they look painted on—are not only unsightly but also uncomfortable, restrictive, and harmful to circulation. Many more designer suits are neither all the one nor the other but some combination of each. With these it is not so much their level of comfort that fails you but their lack of harmony. And still more are neither gargantuan nor mini-malist but marred by some other error. Since these are infinite, they cannot be listed. Yet one sees from experience that only men attired in well-balanced, classic silhouettes ever look smart.

The French and the Swiss looked for many decades rakish and refined. The English look very rakish and very refined. The Ital-ians are an example of past flirtations with disastrous silhouettes. In the 1950s, they became enamored of a minimalist silhouette that, although quickly eliminated in that country, continues to of-fend in our time. Because after crossing the Alps into France, it in-spired a women's couture designer to experiment with men's clothes for the first time. Thus began the era of the menswear de-signer, which swept back into Italy like a plague of locusts, then engulfed the world, and under which we still suffer. In our time most designers are Italian, although the best-dressed men of that nation—even the designers themselves—wear nothing but classic clothing. For this must be noted: no menswear designer has ever worn his own products but always has his clothes made by the world's best bespoke artisans, because he more than anyone knows quality and can afford it. There could be no more damning indictment of designer suits.

So you have to understand that neither harmony with body type nor perfect fit is enough to secure you. For a jacket that fits perfectly but is ridiculous in silhouette is useless, even more so than a jacket tasteful and sophisticated in silhouette that does not fit; for in the latter case it might be altered whereas the former is always harmful. And I spoke of this matter at Nice with a maitre d'hôtel who noticed that the jacket of one of my compan-ions fit badly. For when the maitre d'hôtel said to me that the

Americans do not understand fit, I replied to him that the French do not understand the silhouette, because if they understood they would not wear such square-shouldered, box-hipped, skin-tight jackets. And it may be seen from observation that the greatness of the English and Italians as dressers is caused by their silhouettes, and France's ruin caused by theirs. For the French wear designer suits that are uncomfortable, allow scant freedom of movement and leave little to the imagination. And because of our obsession with fashion they have spread to our shores, and Americans—especially since the 1980s—have succumbed to them in vast numbers; and partly through the ubiquitous wearing thereof has our country been led into sartorial disgrace.

XIII.

Of the Sack, the Continental,
and the Drape

The Sack, which is the other useless silhouette, is wholly unstructured and unfitted. It has no padding, no darts, and no waist suppression but hangs straight from the shoulders. The first mass-produced silhouette, it was designed to fit anyone, with enormous armholes, because those with slight shoulders can fit into large scyes but not the reverse. The trousers of a Sack suit are always unpleated, uncuffed, sit on the hips, and hang straight, effecting the look of an accountant or math teacher. Originated by Brooks Brothers in its heyday, the Sack first found favor with Ivy Leaguers in the 1920s, when it was considered fine for college kids but inappropriate on grown men, who, when they got to Wall Street, were expected to dress with more rigor. Only after the Second World War did the upper class begin wearing it into middle age; and their example made it the silhouette of choice of virtually all Americans in the 1950s and beyond. It is not made much anymore, not even by Brooks Brothers, which has become trendy, but you can still find it at J. Press, a sartorial museum whose styling has not changed since the Eisenhower administration. You can also ascertain its look by watching American films from the '50s, particularly those set in the Northeast; perhaps the most iconic is *The Man in the Gray Flannel Suit*. Even better for grasping the orders of that period is the more recent *Quiz Show,* which had a better costume designer.

Let him, then, who wants to look thoroughly undistinguished and without style wear this silhouette. And though it is less unsightly than the Designer, with either of these ruin is accomplished, for the one looks effeminate and ridiculous while the other imparts no refinement and effects no noble lies. Because the Sack is rarer in our time, it may seem more distinctive; and because the Designer does not lack shape, it may seem more sophisticated. But in truth neither is either, and both must be avoided. In sum, with the Sack, its formlessness is dangerous; with the Designer, its extremity is.

A wise dresser, therefore, has always avoided those silhouettes and turned to the other two. He has preferred to go his own way in wearing a distinctive and refined silhouette not readily available off the rack. And throughout the present era of men's dress one sees that there have been four principle silhouettes that have formed the bases for all variations thereon. And the others are the Continental and the Drape. I shall discuss each in turn, and con-

sider their merits and shortcomings with regard both to comfort
and to style.

The term "Continental" can be and is applied to many
different silhouettes, but for this purpose I mean close-fitting,
non-vented, square- or pagoda-shouldered, highly structured
garments with obsessively clean chests. Also called *"Lo Stile Ital-
iano,"* because it was invented by Roman tailors, it acquired its
other name owing to its great popularity throughout the rest of
Europe. This is the silhouette from which so many of the abom-
inable Designer examples are derived. Yet where the Designer ex-
aggerates the Roman harmonizes. Though it sits close to the body,
it is comfortable, for when it is expertly tailored it nowhere binds
or pulls. Though its shoulders are squarish, or even concave, they
are not extreme or military but well proportioned to their wearer,
and they do not extend beyond the natural shoulderline. Often its
lapels will be shorter and its button stance slightly raised. The
gorge and waist are high. The skirt is close to the hip and the quarters are open. The emphasis is altogether on leanness. One writer
dubbed this silhouette the "power look," for there is never any
creasing, puckering, or wrinkling whatsoever but instead the
cleanest, crispest lines and most precise fit. This is the silhouette
worn by most of the characters in *La Dolce Vita,* and in most
Fellini films, and indeed in most Italian films of that time. The
Roman firm Brioni rose to international reputation on its shoulders. Donald Trump, who is never far from a camera, wears only
this brand, as did Pierce Brosnan in the recent James Bond films.
Though forgettable in every other respect, the opportunity they
afford to see marvelous examples of the Roman silhouette justifies

their rental price. In America, the bespoke tailor Fioravanti has been cutting this silhouette for New York's great personages for half a century.

Similar to this silhouette—but distinctly British rather than Italian—are the Hacking, so called because of its association with equestrian pursuits ("hacking" being an English term for horse riding); the Military, which evolved from British Army uniforms; and the Edwardian, also known as the "Conduit Cut," because its most famous purveyor was a tailor on that London street just north of Savile Row. All are clean and close-fitting like the Continental, but the Hacking and the Military are longer, more broad-shouldered, and wider overall. And of these the Hacking is more angular, with a flared skirt and deep side vents (though true hacking jackets have center vents), whereas the Military is stiffer—some say to better hold up chest medals—and more rounded. Favored by men who like to look imposing in their clothes, these silhouettes are the chief modes of Savile Row. Most of the tailors on that hallowed street make one version or another, but the purest Hacking is considered to be made by Huntsman—famously the most expensive tailor on the Row—and the quintessential Military by Dege, though some might say Gieves & Hawkes. The Edwardian is spare and lean like its namesake made before the Great War, with narrow lapels and drainpipe trousers but modern detailing. It enjoyed a revival among the English after the Second World War, and was immortalized by Sean Connery when he wore it in the early Bond films, and also by Steed in *The Avengers*. But it favors the slender and cannot be worn by anyone whose body mass index exceeds twenty.

The other, and best, silhouette is the Drape. Its origin is English, but its reputation and popularity are international, because it combines the best attributes of the above cuts while avoiding their defects. It is softly constructed but not formless like the Sack. It is shaped at the waist and tapered at the hips but not skin-tight like the Designer. Its shoulders are sloped and unpadded so that they look and feel natural, not stiff and square like the Roman. Most crucially, the jackets are cut with an inch or so of superfluous cloth in the chest and over the shoulder blades: this gives them fullness in the chest while maintaining a slim waist and hips, making you look more muscular and robust. From these innovations— invented in the 1920s and perfected in the '30s by Frederick Scholte, the duke of Windsor's tailor—the Drape silhouette acquired its name. For the extra folds of cloth hang—or "drape"— naturally from the shoulder without structural support, rather than lying smooth against the chest, affixed to a layer of padding. This cloth makes the jacket roomier and thus more comfortable; it allows for greater freedom of movement; and it makes you look less stiff and more nonchalant. But unlike the Sack, the Drape's subtle shaping precludes its looking sloppy; and unlike the Roman, its soft lines preclude its looking studied and effeminate.

Many examples can be adduced to illustrate the greatness of this silhouette. And two of the most excellent are Fred Astaire and Charles, prince of Wales. Astaire wore nothing but this cut, whether as hairy tweed odd jackets or barathea tailcoats. And more than any other man, he demonstrated this silhouette's stylishness and comfort, for he always looked smart and yet wore even the most formal clothes like a pair of pajamas. To see this, one need only screen any of his films, from *Top Hat* to *Funny Face;* for in those days, Hollywood stars (at least the men) wore their own clothes on screen. And you will see with great clarity how rakish and smart his clothes look on his frame; how comfortable he is in them; how nonchalantly he wears them; and how, far from impairing his dancing in any way, he not only has perfect freedom of movement, but after every step, spin, leap, and pirouette they remain perfectly in place. Indeed, it is said that when trying on a new jacket, he used to leap around his tailor's shop, stop suddenly, and check the mirror to make sure his jacket's collar was still flush against his neck. All of these good effects arose from nothing other than the virtue of his clothes' silhouette. In our time, Charles is the most visible representative of the Drape. Because he knows that this cut is shown to greatest advantage double-breasted, all his suits are made in this mode. When you see him, notice above all other factors that subtle amount of superfluous cloth in the chest and blades: that is the drape. And notice how his suit does not look stiff and starchy but always soft and supple.

Despite its superiority to all other silhouettes, the Drape is never found ready-made. The reasons are that it is not popular, because its visible ripples are assumed by the ignorant to be defects; and that it is most difficult to tailor, for "anyone can make a soft jacket if shape is not a consideration, or a shaped one if there's no concern for softness and comfort. The trick is to do both." Few have mastered that trick, and all of them are bespoke tailors. The firm of Anderson & Sheppard in London is the best known, and in America we have Alan Flusser, whose firm makes an Americanized approximation. You can see his clothes in the movie *Wall Street*, for the character of Gekko is dressed throughout in his suits. And I recommend this film most highly for learning about many other aspects of dress, and seeing many excellent examples, though you should only imitate Gekko, because the other characters are either too fashionable or too drab.

The tailors of Naples also make a fine example of the Drape—indeed, many dandies believe that theirs is better than the original and that the Neapolitans are the greatest tailors in the world. The differences are subtle: whereas the English extend the shoulder by about a half inch, the Neapolitans end theirs on the natural shoulderline; whereas the former place the jacket waist about a half inch below the natural waist, the latter place it slightly higher; and they make a jacket that sits closer to the body, the Italians favoring a leaner silhouette than the English. Also, the gorge is higher—so high that on single-breasted jackets the depth of the notch is at the same level as the sleevehead; and the notch itself is slightly upturned. The lapels are a little wider and the quarters more open. The breast pocket (if it is a welt) is curved like a little fishing boat—what they call a *barchetta*. Their patch pockets have a distinct shape, not square but dramatically rounded at the bottom corners and tapered along the sides from bottom to top. But the chief difference is the famous Neapolitan sleevehead, which no one can imitate: a very large opening at the top of the sleeve is carefully hand-pleated into a much smaller scye, making your range of movement most free. On more casual jackets they take this a step further, sewing the shoulder like a shirtsleeve—the famous *spalla camicia*. Small ripples fall from the shoulder seam down into the upper arm, an effect that has been likened to a waterfall. The result is most rounded and relaxed, comfortable for the arm and pleasing to the eye. To get the flavor of the Neapolitan silhouette, you should try on a suit made by La Vera Sartoria, the only competent maker of this style ready-to-wear; but know that most suits made in Naples for the American market are too padded to be authentic. Some believe that the English version of the Drape favors the tall whereas the Neapolitan favors the short, but in truth either will look good on anyone, except the corpulent, who require a clean chest. And whether it is made in Naples by Rubinacci, in Rome or Milan by Caraceni, in London by Anderson, or in New York by Raphael or Shattuck, the Drape is the cut of choice of the world's best-dressed men.

But to return to our matter, most every ready-made suit found in this country—particularly those made by old-line American firms and sold in department stores—are attempts at compromise between the Drape and the Sack, a silhouette that has been termed the "Updated American." It will have padded shoulders and a somewhat suppressed waist but large armholes and little drape. And though this silhouette cannot satisfy a dandy, it is possible to do much worse.

I conclude, thus, that a prudent man will choose one of the above bespoke silhouettes depending on his personal taste, or else, if he is impatient or impoverished, a ready-made of unobjectionable cut. And it has always been the opinion of wise dressers that "the right choice of silhouette can give you years of pleasure; the wrong one will haunt your closet." And the right choice is one that is comfortable without being shapeless and sloppy, and sophisticated without being studied or statuesque; for these factors more than any others make up that elusive quality called "style." And the mode of acquiring it will be easy to find if one reviews the habits of those I have named above and will consider below. For style has nothing or little in common with fashion, and only the unstylish but fashion-conscious profess otherwise.

XIV.

What a Man Should Consider
when Choosing a Garment for Purchase

Thus a dandy should have no other object, nor any other thought, nor take anything else as his art but the art of style and its orders and disciplines; for that is the only art which is of concern to one who wishes to look good. And it is of such virtue that not only does it maintain those who have been born to a tradition of fine dress, but many times it enables men from a modest or indigent state to rise to that rank; and on the contrary, one sees that when the children of stylish fathers have thought more of fashion, frugality, or fitting in than of style, they have squandered their inheritance.

Ronald Reagan, because he learned style, became a first-rate dresser from humble origins in Tampico, Illinois; and his sons, through neglect of it, have sunk to unpresentability despite his example—one because too much in the thrall of fashion, and the other because too little respectful of the dictates of elegance. And among the other causes of evil that being ill dressed brings you, it makes you contemptible, which is one of those infamies any man should be on guard against. For there is no proportion between one who is well dressed and one who is ill dressed, and it is not reasonable that whoever is well dressed respect fully whoever is ill dressed, or that someone ill dressed advance vis-à-vis his better dressed colleagues. For since there is scorn in one and envy in the other, it is not possible for them to work well together; and since bosses prefer to reward those whom they think most redound to the company's glory, those who look bad will not be promoted over those who look good. And they will not, after work in the bar, get the girl, because she will always be more attracted to his better-dressed colleague.

Therefore, a man should never lift his thoughts from considerations of style, and when buying his clothes he should think about it more than when dressing. And he should think about his shape and what flatters it; about proper fit; about avoiding silhouettes that are neither timeless nor rakish; about comfort; about quality and detailing; and about money. Of the first three, I add here only that silhouette can by itself impart great style. For when you are wearing a wardrobe warhorse such as a blazer or gray flannel suit, if it is elegantly cut, you will always look more stylish than the men to the left and right of you who are wearing more lively things badly cut.

In addition, I say that no man is stylish who is uncomfortable in his clothes. You should feel only slightly more constricted in your suits, shirts, and ties than you do in your pajamas; otherwise they either do not fit, are extreme in silhouette, are ill-constructed, or all three. And if you are not comfortable your habits will show it, and far from looking stylish you will look fidgety and irritable.

Detailing can cause some of the same good effects as silhouette, for good tailors do all the little things in a more stylish way, and the sum of these makes for a more elegant whole. The shape of the pocket flaps will mirror the cut of the jacket's front bottom edges: if single-breasted, then gracefully rounded in front, if double, then square; but always coming to a point at the rear, so as to appear rakishly swept back. The breast welt pocket will be angled downward, and the outer edge outward, so as to better sport a handkerchief and avoid bisecting the torso with a horizontal line. All buttonholes will be stitched by hand with silk thread that nearly, but not exactly, matches the "ground," or most prevalent color, of the cloth. And though Wilde may go too far in claiming that "a well-made buttonhole is the only link between art and nature," truly there are few things in this world more beautiful than an expertly handmade buttonhole. The buttons themselves will be made of horn, bone, or corozo (the hard nut of a South American palm tree)—never plastic. The buttons on a jacket's sleeves should kiss—that is, their edges should just touch—and the center of the last button should be no more than an inch and a quarter from the sleeve edge. Every button should be matched with a working buttonhole, even on the jacket's sleeves (though only the vulgar leave these undone). All visible stitching—along the lapels, at the edges of the pockets, on the trouser fly—will be done by hand. Trousers to be worn with suspenders will not have belt loops but either side straps or a back strap made from the suit's cloth and a little metal buckle; and also a waistband extension that extends two and a half to three inches past the fly. These and infinite other details help to enliven a suit made from even the most somber cloth and indicate quality workmanship.

Quality itself is judged chiefly in two modes: by raw materials and construction. Cloth will be discussed in its place; here I note only that while silk for linings may sound luxurious, it is hot and wears out easily. Cooler and more durable is Bemberg, a silk-like synthetic made from the processed linters of cotton plants. Lining in the trousers helps protect delicate cloth from stretching and bagging at the knee or prematurely becoming threadbare, and also shields the legs from scratchy tweeds, but is not necessary in most worsteds. In the best garments the lining is attached by hand so that it moves more fluidly with the wearer. Indeed, the finest garments are made wholly or largely by hand. Certain parts of any jacket must be stitched by hand for it not to be stiff and lifeless, which qualities make it uncomfortable, because it will not move with its wearer, and unsightly, because clothes that look like they are made of cardboard do not look good. And those parts are the collar, the shoulders, the armholes, and the front canvas. All jackets—from the softest Drapes to the stiffest Militaries—are strengthened and given shape by pieces of canvas in the lapels and chest. In the best jackets these are sewn by hand with hundreds of minute stitches, in good ones by machine, and in all others they are not sewn but glued or "fused." Although fusing has improved since its beginnings, nonetheless fused jackets are always stiffer and less breathable and become more so with wear. At worst the glue can dry out, causing the canvas to peel away and the cloth to bubble. Thus dandies always avoid fused jackets, and even machine-canvassed ones, whose lapels never seem to achieve the same "roll"—that graceful bulbousness and arch, like a sail in light wind. To learn what good hand stitching looks like, I can make no better recommendation than for you to examine a garment made by the American firm Oxxford, which makes the best constructed ready-made suits available in our time.

But because hand stitching is expensive, many blanch at paying for it, thinking they can buy two or more garments for the same price as one of higher quality. But you should always buy the best quality garment you can afford, because better garments last longer and look better on you, and in looking better are worn longer. Thus they are cheaper than cheap ones, which are worn briefly and look bad even when new. And let no one resist my opinion on this with that trite proverb, that thrift is the handmaid and nurse of enterprise. For that is true in your dealings with others, where excessive liberality will hurt you. But with regard to your appearance, you should not leave out any part of liberality, because looking shoddy ensures ruin. Yet neither should you overspend on ready-to-wear clothes. For no matter how well made they are or how precisely they fit, they will never be as good as good bespoke. And since the best ready-to-wear clothes cost as much or more than comparable bespoke, it is not reasonable to buy these rather than patronizing a tailor, unless you get them on sale and have no access to any tailors.

I wish to add one further consideration to those I set forth above. And that is that the prudent man is always thinking about what he has and what he needs, and is always hunting for the latter. Thus if he is blessed with a wealth of solid suits, his attention will turn to patterns; if all his shoes are black, he will seek out some in brown; and if he has no checked shirts, he will immediately order one. Above all, he eschews "outfits." For outfits are for women. The well-dressed man never buys any garment that can be worn only with one or few of his other garments, and holds in contempt pre-assembled combinations. Everything you buy should be wearable with most everything you already own. In addition to saving you money, this will make you more stylish, for part of style is knowing how to create different and interesting ensembles from a multitude of garments. Among other praise given to David Niven is that when bespeaking his clothes he never thought of anything but style; and before visiting his tailor or buying a tie, he often reasoned with himself: *What gaps are there in my wardrobe? Would I have more occasion to wear a prince of Wales plaid double-breasted, or a herringbone three-piece? How could I, with one new tie, best employ all of my solid, striped, and checked blue shirts? What pair of shoes could I wear with both a tweed jacket and a winter suit?* And he considered, as he walked London's West End, all of the possibilities that lay before him; he formed opinions and supported them with reasons, so that because of these continued cogitations there could never arise any stylistic opportunity for which he was unprepared.

But those who have not yet learned style should look at photographs and films from the classic era of men's dress, as well as those nearby who dress well, and see how they conduct themselves in things sartorial, and examine the causes of their looking smart and shoddy, so as to be able to avoid the latter and imitate the former. Above all he should do as some excellent man has done in the past who found someone to imitate who had been praised and glorified before him, whose habits and choices he always kept in the forefront of his mind, as they say Astaire imitated Windsor; Gary Cooper, Astaire; and Cary Grant, the illustrations from 1930s issues of *Esquire* and *Apparel Arts*. And whoever examines those pictures will then recognize in the clothing of Grant how much glory that imitation brought him, how much in stylishness, rakishness, and propriety his clothes conformed to what has been depicted in *Apparel Arts* and *Esquire*.

A wise dresser should observe such modes and never succumb either to drab predictability or vulgar showiness, but with his industry and prudence acquire varying garments of consummate style, so that he is always well dressed for every occasion.

XV.

Of Those Things for
Which Men and Especially Dandies
Are Praised or Blamed

It remains now to see what the modes and style of a dandy should be with fabrics, patterns, and colors in particular occasions. And because I know that others have written of this, I fear that in writing of it again, I may be held presumptuous, especially since in disputing this matter I depart from the orders of others. But since my intent is to write something useful to whoever understands it, it has appeared to me more fitting to go directly to the effectual truth of the thing than to the degradation of it. And some have imagined sciences of dressing that look to how clothes are seen by the multitude rather than how they appear in truth; and indeed have written thick books and founded consulting firms that charge usurious sums to advise men that dark solids are safer for business than light colors and bold patterns. But it is so far from how one should dress to how men do dress that he who lets go of what looks good for what the generality finds acceptable ends up looking dull rather than smart. For a man who will make a profession of style in no regard must look dull compared to the few who are stylish. Hence it is necessary for him, if he wants to look good, to learn to be able to be sartorially bold, and to use this and not use it according to necessity.

Thus, leaving out what is prescribed by image consultants and discussing what looks best, I say that all men, and especially dandies, since they dress better, are noted for some quality or two that brings them either blame or praise. And this will have to do with their suits, or their shoes, or shirts, or ties, or their accessories. In the case of most men this is usually some bad habit, like tying one's tie too long or neglecting to polish one's shoes. But for dandies it is an adherence to the time-honored rules of male elegance coupled with a signature trait, like a penchant for brown suede shoes or an unusual daring with respect to hats. And this is why some are considered stylish and others bland; someone colorful, someone drab; someone crisp, someone sloppy; the one harmonious, the other always clashing; the one correct and appropriate, the other vulgar and out-of-place. And I know that everyone will confess that it would be a very laudable thing to find in a man all of the habits of dress that are held good. But because dressing by rote cannot result in style, it is necessary for him to be so prudent as to know for himself how to avoid those vices that make him look shoddy and learn the virtues that make him look stylish. Furthermore, one should not care about incurring notoriety for those habits without which one cannot look good; for if one considers everything well, one will find something held to be correct that if worn would be stultifying, and something else held to be wrong that when worn looks smashing. For truly the verdict of Flusser is golden, which says that the truly stylish man knows enough about the rules to know how and when to break them.

XVI.

Of Suitings

Beginning, then, with the first of the above-mentioned garments, I say that a man's suits are to his wardrobe what his home is to his life. This is not so much because they are the most important part of any ensemble, nor even owing to their great expense—greater than any other part of the typical wardrobe—but to their status as the uniform of business. Just as a man lives in his house at night and on weekends, so may he be said to live in his suits during the week.

How this came to be is notable. All of the tailored clothing we wear today derives from some ancient compromise between garments once worn by Englishmen at their country estates and those worn for some ceremonial purpose in town. What we would recognize as a suit was born in the mid-19th century, when men began to wear ensembles in which coat, vest, and trousers were all made from the same cloth (and hence the term "suit," which is derived from the French *suivre,* "to follow"). In this they differed from all hitherto existing male attire, it being more expensive, and thus considered more elegant, to have garments made from different cloths. The first suits were called "lounge suits" because compared to their more formal brethren they were so loose-fitting and softly constructed that they were thought fit only for lounging. Thus they were strictly leisure wear, made from thick cloths suitable for the rigors of the outdoors, and worn only in the country. But men came to love them and desired to take them to town, and so began having them made in dark, smooth cloths, these being more reminiscent of the frock coat. At first they wore them only in the park or else to their clubs and other venues where ladies were not present. But they could not long resist wearing them for business, and relegated the frock coat to formal occasions, and soon after gave it up altogether. And from London the suit spread throughout Europe, then to America, and then around the world, until it became the international standard for correct male attire. But lest you think that this makes it drab or square, remember that the foremost avatars of cool in the last century, the great jazz musicians, wore it routinely.

Suits may be single- or double-breasted, as was said, single being more common but double more stylish. They may also be two- or three-piece. Pepys records that vests—also called waistcoats—were invented by Charles II as a way of supporting English cloth weavers during a trade war with Holland, and also to assert his freedom from Louis, king of France, who during

Charles' exile had not only housed and fed him, but forced him to wear effeminate clothes. Some even trace the beginning of the suit to Charles' decree of October 8, 1666, mandating that vests be worn at court. This opinion has certain reasons that at a distance appear true but are altogether alien from the truth. For those garments were still festooned with too much frippery to be considered the modern suit's ancestor, which arose a century and a half later when Brummell brought country attire to town. The first suits were all three-piece, but hot weather made the two-piece popular, and the sumptuary laws of the Second World War made it ubiquitous. Yet vests are still favored by dandies, but in summer only by masochists, and with double-breasted suits only if you get cold easily or are afraid to show your suspenders. Most vests are single-breasted and have four welt pockets and six buttons, the bottom button never being fastened. Some say that this custom came to be when Bertie, prince of Wales (Victoria's son), overindulged at a meal and undid the bottom button of his vest to relieve pressure on the royal girth, and his entourage sycophantically followed suit. His grandson the duke of Windsor disputes this, arguing that the practice arose from a mistake. Whatever the truth, it caught on, and bespoke tailors have since cut single-breasted vests so that the bottom button cannot be buttoned at all but is purely decorative. Single-breasted vests generally do not take lapels, but those with sportier suits may have short notched lapels. Those made in Savile Row will have an extra buttonhole, oriented vertically between the fourth and fifth buttonholes, to convey a watch chain. Double-breasted vests—like the one Steve McQueen wore to the art auction in *The Thomas Crown Affair*—though rare, are beloved by dandies. These take six buttons, arranged like a keystone, with the three on the right always fastened. Because of the lower buttoning point, they have a deeper front than single-breasted vests and thus show more shirt and tie. They are correct only with single-breasted suits and must have lapels, either shawl or peak; and if shawl, the jacket lapels may be either notched or peaked; but if peaked, the jacket lapels must match. Whether its vest is single- or double-breasted, a three-piece suit should always have high-rise trousers that take suspenders, because exposing waistband or shirt is ungentlemanly and unpardonable, and belts under vests cause an unsightly bulge.

With respect to cloth, there is only one unbreakable rule: suitings (what the trade calls cloth for suits) must be made solely from natural fibers; as indeed must all cloth, for any garment. This does not ensure good cloth, but the opposite precludes it. And the best and most widely available cloth for suitings is wool, which breathes easily, tailors well, resists wrinkles, holds dyes, and can be made in a variety of weaves and weights. Wool cloth is made chiefly in two modes: either the fibers are combed out flat and straight and then spun in a precise and orderly way to make worsted yarns; or the combing process is skipped, resulting in woolen yarns. Tailors refer to how a cloth feels as its "hand." Woolens are fuzzy and spongy (or "lofty," as the tailors say), and generally thicker and heavier than worsteds, which are thinner and crisper. And worsteds may be dense and silky-smooth, like gabardine, or porous and dry, like fresco, a coarse yet loose and breathable weave perfect for summer. Other notable worsted weaves include barathea and sharkskin. Yet the most common by far is the plain weave, also called "four harness" after the name of the loom on which it is made. Tweeds, Saxonies, and most flannels are woven from woolen yarns in a purposefully haphazard and imprecise fashion, yet flannels can also be made from worsted yarns, making them more hard-wearing but less lofty and distinctive. Also, worsteds can be left with a fuzzy surface rather than being "clear cut," a process much like running a lawn mower over the cloth to give it a smooth surface. "Worsted flannels" and "unfinished worsteds" often look so similar that only weavers and cloth merchants can tell the difference. Beyond wool, linen (made from the flax plant) and mohair (shorn from Angora goats) make fine summer suitings, but the former wrinkles easily and the latter shines like satin and cracks like plaster unless it is blended with wool. Cotton suits—in poplin or seersucker—are popular in America, but Europeans do not wear them. Worsted cashmere for winter is popular with plutocrats, as this delicate cloth wears out after minimal wearings and only they can afford to replace it regularly. Dandies enjoy silk, but only the rough, matte-finished weave known as dupioni; shiny silk is for gangsters.

Cashmere is the most expensive material for suitings, cotton the cheapest, wool in the middle. But the quality of wool varies widely, so that the most expensive can cost more than cashmere. Its cost is determined in part by the width of its individual fibers: the narrower they are, the costlier the cloth. Width is properly denoted by micron number but more commonly by "Super" number. Many conflate this with "thread count," but that term is not used for suitings. In the wool markets of Yorkshire, "count" signifies the utmost number of "hanks"—a spool totaling 560 yards of yarn—that can be spun from one pound of raw wool; hence a pound of 80s count wool can be spun into 80 hanks of yarn. The thinner the raw fibers, the more hanks that can be spun from them and the silkier the resulting cloth, hence the higher cost. Decades ago, the spinners Joseph Lumb & Sons began awarding the honorific "Golden Bale" to the raw wool they judged to be the finest brought to market in a given year. This always commanded the highest prices and made up into the most luxurious goods ("goods" being another way the fabric trade refers to cloth). For years, nothing finer than 80s (about 19.5 micron) was ever seen and many assumed that nothing finer could be grown. But advances in breeding yielded sheep with ever finer fleeces. And when the first 100s count wool won the Golden Bale award the merchants were so astounded that, in a fit of exuberance, they dubbed it "Super 100s." Soon the Italian weavers in Biella got wind of this advance and saw a niche. They spent millions developing high-tech looms that could rapidly mass produce low micron goods in the lightest possible weights without breaking the fibers. Their marketing minions hyped this cloth by designating ever-lower micron numbers with ever-higher "Super" numbers, with every decade of "Super" number representing half a micron. Specializing in this stuff, they amassed huge fortunes selling to designers and preying on the uninformed. For while the finest "Supers" are undoubtedly soft to the touch, so are they often too delicate to hold a crease or stand up even to ordinary wear. At their upper reaches—and as the arms race between ranchers and weavers and retailers rages on, we have already seen "Super 250s," and many believe it will not end until some marketing genius claims to have loomed the first zero micron "Super 450s" and sells it for the highest price ever paid for wool—they are so delicate that they should be avoided by anyone not rich enough to treat his suits as disposable. Dandies prefer traditionally woven cloth (whether made in England or by the few Italian firms that weave the English way) with more body and real heft, and avoid the "Supers" altogether, except those made for uncompromising firms, such as H. Lesser. For there is more to quality than micronage: one must consider the length, strength, and elasticity of the fibers—the best of which come from the Merino sheep of Australia—and also the weaving and finishing of the cloth. Indeed, the best goods designated Golden Bale today are not stratospheric "Supers" but wool with counts in the low hundreds that is selected, spun, woven, and finished according to far higher standards than those prevailing among the makers of the über-supers. In addition, all decent yarns are two-ply: that is, each individual yarn is actually two twisted tightly together. The best suitings are "two-by-two," in which both the warp, or lengthwise yarns, and the weft, the crosswise yarns, are two-ply. These cloths are smoother and more lustrous, because they are denser, and more durable; for, the yarns being stronger, they break less often and do not pill. Some mills make cloth with three- or even four-ply yarns; and while this can be most excellent, it is more often stiff and uncomfortable; whereas two-by-two construction is almost always good enough.

Cloth is weighed in ounces per running yard, or else in grams per running meter—"running" being the industry term for uncut cloth's width inside the selvage (the woven edges that prevent fraying). English cloth is typically woven in 60 inch goods, Continental 150 centimeters, and old-fashioned tweeds 30 inches. Cloth is usually about two inches, or five centimeters, narrower inside the selvage. Tailors' swatches will denote a cloth's weight on a small sticker. Most ready-made suits will not convey this information, requiring you to guess based on how it feels. The lightest cloths are seven or eight ounces—godsends in torrid climates but useless elsewhere—while the heaviest can weigh more than twenty ounces, most excellent for the bitter cold. Nine- to eleven-ounce cloth is most suitable for temperate climates, and is the most versatile. Heavy cloth is easier to tailor and hangs like steel, rarely wrinkling, while lighter cloth in inexpert hands tailors into a puckered and sloppy-looking finished garment. Yet the best light-weight tropical worsteds of today are woven from yarns twisted so tightly that they tailor like cloth twice their weight while losing none of their airiness. This and other innovations make for what the industry calls "high-tech" fabrics; these are used mostly for ready-to-wear garments because they tailor more easily, are made in the more popular lighter weights, and can be cut in bulk by machine without much spoilage. But bespoke tailors who cut and sew by hand prefer to work with cloths made in the traditional manner, such as flannels from the West of England, worsteds from Huddersfield, and tweeds from Scotland.

Gray, blue, and brown are the great triumvirate of colors for men's suitings—none but these should be worn. The only exceptions are olive and off-white, and these only in warm weather. The darker its color, the more formal a suit. Lighter shades go well with warmer weather while darker shades are appropriate all year. Brown in any shade, from tan to chocolate to charcoal, is best worn during the day, as are lighter shades of blue and gray. Some hold fast to the ancient rule "no brown in town" and claim this color should only be worn in the country. Yet the only authoritative canon of men's style—1930s issues of *Apparel Arts*—frequently depicts men in brown town suits. If this were not enough, in 1993 the Federation of Merchant Tailors in London officially declared this rule dead. Still valid, however, is the rule which holds that solid black is too severe for suitings. Hipsters and celebrities denounce this rule and even deny its existence, thinking themselves sartorial Supermen above the strictures that bind the multitude; but these men deceive themselves, and their hubris often produces the very errors the rules exist to prevent. For my part, I do not deny their right to wear black suits; I assert only that in doing so they look bad. For black either overwhelms or overvivifies other colors. This is desirable for women and perhaps for professional sports uniforms. But gentlemen understand that on men it looks oily. Light gray or white stripes can make a black ground look gray but the black makes the stripes glow like neon. These are popular in chest-thumping environs like the mafia and the counting houses of the City of London but *outré* anywhere else. As for patterns, solids are the most formal, followed by stripes, nailhead, and birdseye (tiny, frequent dots on a darker background; nailhead is smaller and squarer), pic-and-pic (tiny, staggered diagonal lines, like miniature staircases), herringbone, windowpane, houndstooth, and glen plaid. Although there are other patterns that are very stylish and favored by dandies, only the above are always safe for business.

To the modes of employing these various kinds of suitings, I want to adduce two examples that have displayed themselves within our memory; and these are George H. W. Bush and Willie Brown. President Bush dressed every day in similar suits, all dark gray or blue worsteds, and earned great credit with the people, or at least avoided offending them, because the citizens of democracies do not like ostentatious dress in their leaders. On the other hand, Brown, former Mayor of San Francisco, always wears a variety of suitings with great panache and to great effect, and indeed does all those things that should be done by a prudent and virtuous man to look his best. And because he was elected in San Francisco, his dandification not only did not harm him, but added to his glory, because San Franciscans esteem themselves superior to the multitude and think they deserve to be led by one of exceptional style. Thus if one considers all the habits of the mayor, one will come to understand the modes in which suitings should be employed, which I do not judge superfluous to discuss; for I do not know what better teaching I could give to an aspiring dandy than the example of his habits. And if ultimately his wardrobe is incomplete because he never wears anything but worsteds, it is not his fault, but arises from a great malignity of fortune—namely that he lives in warm, sunny California, where flannels and tweeds are not only useless but harmful.

The mayor does not leave out any colors or patterns. One sees him not only in browns, blues, and grays, and all shades thereof— tan, taupe, and chocolate; slate, harbor, and navy; and Cambridge, charcoal, and gunmetal—but also in more adventurous colors such as blue-gray and lovat. One also sees him in solids, glen-plaids, nailheads, houndstooths, windowpanes, miniature checks, herringbones, and overplaids, as well as pin-, chalk-, pencil-, roped-, and beaded-, single-, double-, triple-, and even four-bar cluster stripes (also a favorite of Wall Street maven Lawrence Kudlow). And this is owing not only to his infinite good taste, but also to his firmly established position, since for many years he has had both the means and the inclination to build a fine wardrobe.

But I recommend that the aspiring dandy begin with the basics and move on to the more unusual and esoteric patterns and colors only after he has secured for himself the foundation of a fine wardrobe. And this means that above all he should have a solid gray worsted suit, medium to dark—but not so dark that it makes you look like an undertaker, and not so light that it cannot be worn by one. For there is virtually no occasion—business, ceremonial, or social—for which a gray suit is not correct. And a gray suit is most versatile with respect to shirts, ties, and accessories. It can be worn with almost any color or pattern, and is easily dressed up for formal occasions and down for informal ones. And the next suit he acquires should be a solid navy worsted. Because it is darker than medium gray, it is useful for evenings, for such occasions as concerts, shows, and dinner parties. And because it is not neutral but colored, it looks smarter in daylight than the gray worsted. It too responds to infinite shirt and tie combinations and can be dressed up or down according to the convenience of the wearer. Beyond these two essential garments, one should acquire still more solid suits before moving on to patterns. I recommend at least a tan fresco for summer and a mid-gray flannel for winter. And when the time comes to expand your wardrobe into the realm of patterns, choose the classics first—those mentioned above—and the unusual and esoteric later. For whoever buys busy and colorful patterns to the exclusion of all others is ruined. For since these can be worn with so few shirts and ties, he will be forced to wear the same ones over and over and thus look the same every day; and men who always look the same look contemptible and ridiculous. Also, these suits force you to buy shirts and ties that go only with them and no others, whereas you ought to buy shirts and ties that go with as many of your suits as possible, as was said above and will be discussed at length below. And they are useless or even harmful for occasions that call for subdued, subtle attire. Yet one sees many men who own nothing but unusual, esoteric suits who think that because their suits are different, they look smart, whereas in truth they look dull. This error is especially common among the young, as was said.

And these were the mayor's arrangements for building his wardrobe. He began with solids, first with blue and gray and then on to brown and tan and other colors and shades. He moved next to classic patterns, all the while still wearing his solids when necessary or when he fancied them, while mixing in the patterns at his pleasure. He then began to acquire more unusual and esoteric patterns, like nailhead with an overplaid, or double-bar pencil stripes. He varied the weight of his suits, buying heavy worsteds for winter, frescos and linens and mohairs for summer, and gabardines and sharkskins for spring and fall. Not only does this provide more variety and make him look smarter, it extends the life of his suits, since each are worn only in season and thus much less than so-called "10-month" fabrics which are worn ubiquitously and so wear out faster. Now the mayor is prepared for every occasion; he can effect any look or level of formality he wants and can wear unusual and esoteric patterns to great effect because he does not do so every day; and yet even in solids he looks smart by any measure, and certainly by comparison with those around him.

And because this point is deserving of notice and of being imitated by others, I do not want to leave it out. Once the mayor took office, he found City Hall populated by ill-dressed laggards and ruffians long accustomed to wearing whatever they pleased, and who had sunk so low as to wear not merely bad suits but in many cases no suit at all. Since he understood that wherever business is conducted, those who transact it must dress accordingly, and that where men do not, business suffers, he judged it necessary to enact a strict dress code to reduce the bureaucracy to orderliness and obedience to the mayoral arm. So he forced the malcontents under his employ to upgrade their appearance and imperiled all who refused. The shock of seeing long-time colleagues threatened for their shoddy dress, and the relief at not being among them, left the remainder at once satisfied and stupefied. And although this may not have improved the substance of civic administration in that city, it has at least improved the appearance thereof.

But let us return to where we left off. The virtue of the mayor's suits extends beyond their tasteful colors and rakish patterns. They are also of flattering and elegant silhouette, they fit impeccably, are made of the finest cloths, and are most superior in quality. Moreover, he takes excellent care of them: he has them dry-cleaned as infrequently as possible, because that process shortens the life of any garment; he always brushes and hangs them after every wearing; and he steams them when excessive wrinkles make them unsightly. Thus when I sum up all the habits of the mayor, I do not know how to reproach him; on the contrary, it seems to me he should be put forward, as I have done, to be imitated by all those who desire to look their best. One could only indict him in not having any woolen suits; for, as was said, one should have suits in a variety of cloths as well as colors and patterns. And although he lived for so long in hot, dry Sacramento, now that he is back in cool and breezy San Francisco he should include flannels and tweeds in his wardrobe. So the mayor errs in this choice and it is the cause of his wardrobe's ultimately falling short of perfection.

XVII.

Of Footwear, and Whether
It Is Better to Buy Italian Than English,
or the Contrary

Descending next to the other garments cited before, I say that if suits are to a man's wardrobe as a house is to his life, then shoes are akin to his car. And the reasons are that they are the second most expensive part of any wardrobe, and the most telling measure of a man's taste. For just as vulgar men drive ostentatious cars and careless men wrecks, so vulgar men love gaudy footwear while sloppy, indifferent dressers wear shoes that are cheaply made and badly kept. And the latter error is by far the more common; for he who observed that because men rarely see their own feet, few bother about what is on them, spoke the truth. But, as columnist George Frazier is said to have said, "Wanna know if a guy is well dressed? Look down." Whoever looks down at the feet of David Letterman or Donald Rumsfeld will see sneakers, even when they are wearing suits. This cannot be called an error, since it is so uncouth that even they must know the violence they are doing to their own appearance and to good taste. But I will confine myself to shoes dignified enough to be worn with tailored clothing.

Last is to shoes what silhouette is to suits. The word literally means the wooden model of a foot around which a shoe is built. But cordwainers (these are people who make shoes from scratch using only some leather, hemp twine, cork, and nails; cobblers only do repairs) also use it to refer generally to a shoe's shape. The foot being an ungainly thing, wise men seek out shoes that minimize its appearance. Bespoke shoes will always fit and feel best, because they are made on lasts carved to the exact requirements of actual feet. Most dandies believe that they also look better even though, by conforming so closely to the shape of your foot, they look quirky when compared to a standardized ready-made shoe. But their sculpted uniqueness is part of their charm; and in their greater precision, there is less of them, so they will always look smaller than ready-made shoes on the same feet. The best of these latter are made on lasts that also minimize the foot. To assess a last's quality, first look at the shoe from above: if the outside line is curved, the inside line is reasonably straight, and you cannot see the edges of the sole peeking out along the sides, turn the shoe over; if the outside line looks roughly the same as it does from above, while the inside line of the sole is sharply concave at the waist (the narrowest part of a shoe) so that the shoe almost looks curved like a banana, then chances are the shoe has been made on a good last. Toe shape affects the look of a shoe, but its comfort hardly at all. Square toes can minimize the appearance of long feet but look clunky. More elegant is the "chisel"—pioneered by master cordwainer George Cleverley—which has a squarish front but flat, angled sides and a sloping top. The rounded toe is more common; it looks best when its inside edge is nearly parallel to the foot while its outside edge is more angled. Pointed toes are for women.

It is universally acknowledged that proper shoes are either black or brown. Other colors are seen but their legitimacy is disputed. Americans love burgundy (also called "oxblood") but the English sneer at it. Italians wear tan in town all year whereas the English wear it only in summer and only on holiday. Dandies love white but the generality are afraid of it. The French will wear anything—even blue and green—though the most elegant among them know better. Shoes are more or less formal depending on their shade, black being the most formal and white the least. The most revered rule concerning shoes states that they should never be lighter than the trouser. This is a good rule for beginners or for those who must avoid offending important, hidebound men. But dandies know that brown shoes are much smarter than black (for color is always more interesting than its absence) even when paired with the darkest shades of blue and gray, provided they are made from fine leather, and well-polished. The Italians love brown shoes so much that they do not even make black shoes. Flusser records that, among Americans, the Bostonians have long preferred brown to black, and their example is imitated by the best dressed among their countrymen. Nonetheless, black shoes are essential, as they alone are appropriate for grave occasions or when doing business with Englishmen, who adhere to them as a matter of religious faith. White is very stylish and dandified, but appropriate only in summer, and only with light-weight, light-colored cloths (especially linen and seersucker), or else with a blue blazer and white trousers. A more versatile option is London tan—a rich, orangish light brown that is the perfect complement to spring and summer suitings, or to any suiting worn in warmer months. Very dandified, but not at all versatile, are "co-respondents" or "spectator shoes"; that is, shoes made in two colors. The classic version has a white suede vamp (the part that covers the top of the foot) and a brown toe cap, heel counter, and throat; though sometimes tan or olive linen is substituted for the white suede, which is nearly impossible to clean. Spectators were once worn with great panache by all the best dressers, but today are seen hardly at all because of their flashiness and because polishing them is so nerve-wracking. They can be worn only with less formal clothes and only to informal, outdoor events, and are perhaps best left to the golf course and the race track.

Concerning leather, I say that good shoes are made from calf-skin, which is durable yet supple, breathable yet insulating, and can hold a shine. This should always be the result of wax and spit and effort. "Corrected grain" leathers that have been scraped, sanded, and bathed in chemicals to create a plastic-looking perma-shine should be avoided. Dandies enjoy suede, which in brown not only goes with everything but goes best with anything. Some wear none but this, and have a dozen pairs in differing shades and models. Astaire favored them above all other shoes, partly because their supreme comfort made dancing easier (for suede is more pliant than other leathers), partly because their matted surface makes feet look smaller, but mostly because of their superior elegance.

And I wish Astaire to suffice as an example for all considerations concerning footwear; for not only did he always wear his with consummate style, but because he did so much dancing in his films, directors always shot him so that you can see his feet. Finer suedes are made from buckskin, though reverse calf is more common. Acceptable shades range in hue from ginger to tobacco to chocolate. White is the only other acceptable color for suede. Indeed, white shoes should only be buckskin suede, as should the white portions of co-respondents. Shoes made from heavier skins go best with flannels and tweeds. Cowhide takes well to embossing with patterns like pebble-grain, which makes a fine country shoe. Cordovan, which is not a skin but a membrane from the rump of a horse, is the most durable leather of all, but its warmth makes it impractical for summer. Unlike calf, which looks fake in burgundy, cordovan responds marvelously to this dye. The oxblood cordovan shoe was a staple of American dress in the 1950s, and has since spread to the rest of the world, though the English still resist it. The finest examples are made by the Spanish and the Hungarians, but the American firm Alden remains the best-known purveyor. Dandies (who by nature patronize a bespoke cordwainer) will come across other, more exotic leathers. The most common is crocodile, favored by the extravagant, although rarer skins such as pigskin, Russian reindeer, and even bullfrog will occasionally be seen. It is impossible to give rules as to which are acceptable, except that gaudy, ostentatious skins like stingray and ostrich are appropriate only for cowboy boots, and these should never be worn with suits, not even in Texas.

Furthermore, dress shoes are either lace-ups or slip-ons. The former are formal, the latter informal; though among these, dress slip-ons—shoes with vamps so high they look like lace-ups without lacing—are formal enough for suits and designed to be worn with them. Popular with the English, these will have elastic gussets on the sides or under the vamp to allow for a snugger fit. But they are almost unknown in America. What we think of as a slip-on the English consider casual wear or else deride as a refuge for the lazy. The father of these is the shoe once worn by fishermen in Norway, called the "Norwegian peasant slipper." Americans call it the "loafer," or sometimes the "penny loafer," a name it acquired in the 1950s when students at Northeastern prep schools took to inserting coins into the little slot in the saddle. But unless you are making an ironic comment on the decline of the WASP upper class or are named Chip or Biff, I recommend against this. And although loafers with metal decorations over the vamp have gained wide acceptance in our time, the only metal a dandy will allow to interrupt the sublime visage of polished leather is the buckle on a monk-strap. The tassel loafer, denounced by George Bush as effete and elite, was invented by Americans after the Second World War, and is today popular throughout the world. Americans—ignoring the sneers of the English—consider it formal enough to be worn with suits. Without condoning the practice, I caution that care be taken to wear only those of the highest quality, and only in dark colors. Because loafers are made by everyone, quality ranges from dismally styled and shoddily constructed to examples that are the equal of any shoe made anywhere. Some are deliberately made to be worn more with chinos than with tailored clothing, and these must be avoided. One test is whether it has leather soles and heels; for, aside from white bucks, no shoe acceptable for wear with a tie will ever be made with rubber soles. Suit and shoe should also be in proportion to one an-other: dainty tassel loafers are overwhelmed by heavy cheviots; and when trying to project formality or gravity, only lace-ups will do.

These are made in two modes: either they have open lacing, in which the two sides drawn together by the laces are sewn over the vamp, or they have closed lacing, in which those sides are sewn under the vamp. Americans call the former bluchers and the latter balmorals, but this is misleading. The English are more precise, calling the former derbies and the latter oxfords, as balmorals (or "bals") are a type of oxford with straight side seams, derived from the dress boot popular in the days when city streets were awash in mud and horse manure. Oxfords with a throat shaped like the let-ter U and no side seams are called "adelaides"; and those made of a single piece of leather are called "wholecuts." Bluchers, because they are bulkier than the sleek oxford, are less formal. Among their many virtues, they are more comfortable on those with high arches, can help give mass to tiny feet, and go well with bulky cloth. But they should be avoided by those with large feet, and all but the sleekest examples look out of place with smooth, light worsteds.

Lace-ups may be left plain or decorated in a variety of modes. The most common is to sew superfluous pieces of leather onto the outside of the shoe; and the most exalted of these is the toe-cap. The cap-toed shoe most benefits those with large feet, as the cap cuts across the middle of the vamp, deëmphasizing length. But it is essential for everyone because it is the quintessential suit shoe (and indeed can only be worn with suits); and in black, without any broguing, it is the most formal of all business shoes. All men must have a pair, as these alone are appropriate for the gravest occasions. Broguing—small, decorative holes punched along the seams—decreases the formality of a shoe but adds character. The practice is said to have originated on the Scottish and Irish moors, where men punched holes in their shoes to let water drain out. Some shoemakers refer to models by the amount of broguing, so that "punched caps" will have perforations just along the toe-cap seam, "quarter brogues" along the toe-cap and side seams, "half brogues" add a medallion design perforated into the cap, and "three-quarter brogues" include a perforated "counter" (a decorative piece of leather above the heel).

The "full brogue" has perforations along every seam, from toe to heel. The Americans call it a "wing tip" because the toe decoration, instead of being straight, comes to a point and is said to resemble the wing of a bird. During the Second World War, when tight restrictions were placed on leather usage, English shoemakers offered full brogues without broguing, called "austerity brogues." Their distinctively sleek lines ensured their survival beyond the war, and they remain popular with dandies as an alternative to the plain cap toe. With all its broguing and superfluous leather, the true full brogue is not the best shoe for those with large feet, but it goes well with heavier cloths, making it a useful winter shoe, especially when made in cordovan. In the 1950s cordovan wing tips were a fetish among Ivy League Northeasterners; everyone who wasn't wearing tassel loafers with their dark worsted Sack suits was wearing these. By contrast, the English have always regarded the brogue as a country shoe and the Italians have taken to it only recently. Another countrified shoe is the split-toe or Norwegian shoe—not the Norwegian peasant slipper but a lace-up which, though bereft of broguing, is as bulky as the full brogue because of its shape, and so is proper only with suits of flannel or tweed, or odd jackets and trousers.

Neither a lace-up nor a slip-on, the monk-strap is a blucher that closes via a strap and buckle. In its classic form, it is plain-toed and bereft of broguing. Dandies have always favored this mode, owing to its panache and rarity, but also because its plain front shows to advantage an expanse of finely polished, mottled brown leather, like a pair of ancient bespoke riding boots. Although a blucher, its sleekness minimizes the foot, making it suitable for lightweight cloths and slim silhouettes. The French favor a version with two straps and a toe cap, while the Italians often make it encrusted with an abundance of decoration that clutters its clean lines.

Most any of the above models can also be made as dress boots. These are wonderful for adverse weather, for they protect the ankle and foot from precipitation and reduce the hazards of slushy streets. Dress boots often take soles of double thickness for additional durability, and add a layer of rubber to keep out water. Yet made on a proper last, they are indistinguishable from shoes when their tops are concealed by your trouser legs.

Dress shoes are constructed in one of two modes: either the sole is stitched to the "upper," or body, of the shoe; or else it is glued. Stitching is as old as shoemaking itself. Gluing was introduced by the Italian makers of bespoke shoes for female aristocrats and movie stars. Since women like their feet to look as small as possible, these cordwainers used very thin leather and as little as possible, leaving out insoles, inner linings, and even stitching twine. Later, when they began making men's shoes, they made models that complemented the minimalist Continental silhouette, using these same techniques. For many years these were all they made, until the so-called Bologna-construction method—in which the sole is stitched directly to the upper—rose to ascendancy. This is slightly more durable than gluing, but still makes a light and flexible shoe. Later, they began adding insoles, making a so-called "Blake-stitched" shoe that was still light but slightly more durable yet. The English, by contrast, have always used a welt—a separate strip of leather that is stitched to the upper, with the sole stitched to it. The finest shoes, and nearly all bespoke shoes, are still welted by hand. But the modern shoe industry was born when the American Charles Goodyear, son of the man who first vulcanized rubber, invented a machine that could do it quickly and cheaply. This process was perfected by the English during the First World War, when the shoe factories of Northampton had to turn out millions of pairs of boots durable enough to withstand the rigors of trench warfare.

From this a dispute arises whether it is better to buy Italian than English, or the reverse. The response used to be that one would want to buy English, since welted shoes are more durable, hence they last longer, and are more substantial, hence they better complement masculine clothes; whereas sleek, slim Bologna- and Blake-stitched shoes look beautiful on female feet but ridiculous on male ones. Glued soles are always an abomination.

But in our time not all well-made, well-styled shoes are English; for although the classic models discussed above were invented by the English, the Italians now make some of the best examples, and the Italian shoe industry has by and large moved away from the dainty and effeminate toward the masculine and classic. And the Hungarians, the Spanish, the Japanese, some Americans, and even the French are now making good shoes, so that what you must look for is not so much English provenance but English styling and construction. Know well, however, that many English, most American, and some Italian shoes are made on overlarge lasts, with double soles and an excess of decorative leather. Favored by club kids and would-be bohemians, these shoes make average feet look huge and overwhelm all but the heaviest cloths and fullest silhouettes. Shoes that adhere to the middle path go best with the Drape and with most American silhouettes; and since these shoes were invented by the English, and are still made mostly by them, it is always safer to buy English.

Except in the case of socks. All well-dressed men, and especially dandies, take great care in selecting their socks, and wear only high-quality, single-fabric, sized, patterned examples. All good dress socks are made from either cotton or wool (although a small amount of nylon helps them stay up and extends their life). Cotton is finer and more lustrous than wool, and also cooler, and its sheen matches the smoothness of tropical worsteds; while wool insulates better, is more durable, and its fuzziness complements winter's nubbier suitings. Well-dressed men never wear socks made from a blend of both, for these being neither the one nor the other, lack the virtues of either: neither warm in winter nor cool in summer, not fine, not durable, not attractive. Most American socks are blends, and all are one-size-fits-all, something no dandy can consider. Rare is the manufacturer who still makes socks in various sizes (and for some mysterious reason, your sock size is always a size and a half larger than your shoe size). These are not only more comfortable but more seemly, because socks that are too small must stretch so that they are transparent like a woman's stocking, and socks that are too large fall and bunch around the ankle. But you are more likely to find socks sized S, M, L, and XL, each letter corresponding to a small range of shoe sizes; and these will adequately fit most any foot. Nearly all of the single-fabric, sized socks available today are made by the Italians; and no men wear socks with greater panache—especially the Neapolitans, who used to bespeak even their hose. The English made and wore fine socks until hard times forced on them what Michael Lewis called "the sort of sagging thin black socks I came to recognize as a symbol of Britain's long economic decline." The decline has been reversed, but—with the exception of one manufacturer—their socks are still dreck. Turning to how you should wear them, an ancient rule holds that socks should match the trouser not the shoe. But dandies understand that, used prudently, socks can bridge the gap between shoe and cuff; used virtuously, they can make a sly reference to something worn above the waist. Above all, no dandy ever wears solid socks, for that is stylistic surrender. The best dressers understand that since shoes are nearly always solid, and trousers often are, patterned socks break up the monotony. Patterns may be of many diverse kinds, but the most useful are polka dots, herringbone, birdseye, windowpane, glen plaid, and small checks. Funky, irregular, or brilliantly colored patterns should be avoided. The larger the pattern's scale, the less formal the sock; and less formal patterns, such as argyle, should never be worn with smooth worsteds, for the same reason that fine weaves, such as cotton lisle, should not be worn with heavy, informal cloths. The dandy's favorite sock pattern has always been the clock, a narrow decoration that runs up each side of the sock, forming an angle at the ankle which makes it look like the hands of a clock. Long a specialty of the French, especially in cotton lisle, it is difficult to find in our time but remains as stylish as ever. Most patterned socks will be of two colors—three or more is rare; rarer still is the ability to recognize those that are acceptable. But this can be learned and you must learn it; for nothing more enlivens a man's appearance at so little cost than an adventurous yet tasteful pair of socks. Never wear socks that do not extend over your calf, for the curve of the muscle helps hold them up, and nothing looks more vulgar and contemptible than bare skin peeking out between trouser cuff and sock.

I conclude, then, that in the case of shoes it is better to buy English, for a man's shoes should complement the manliness, timelessness, and unimpeachable quality of his clothes; whereas in the case of socks it is better to buy Italian, because these are not only the best examples, but also the most readily available in our time.

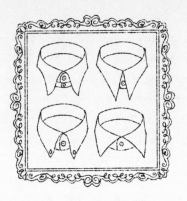

XVIII.

In What Mode Shirtings
Should Be Employed

How laudable it is for a man to wear tasteful, handsomely made, well-fitting shirts everyone understands. Nonetheless one sees in our time many men wearing vulgarly styled, cheaply constructed, ill-fitting shirts, or else never deviating from one mode and color. I say that the latter error is caused either by fear or sloth. The fear is derived from men's not wishing to stand out or be thought vain or effeminate. As for sloth, blue and especially white shirts are sold everywhere, go with everything, and require no effort to acquire or wear. But men who adhere to this mode doom themselves to staidness and forgo the most useful means of attaining style. For not only are there many more acceptable patterns and colors for shirts than for suits, but shirts are much less expensive, so that it is possible greatly to diversify one's wardrobe through the judicious purchase thereof, whereas buying a similar number of suits would ensure ruin. Well-dressed men possess a vast multitude of shirts in all patterns and colors, whereas they might have as few as a dozen suits. But all those shirts bring such versatility to those few suits that such a wardrobe is capable of infinite variations and combinations.

Because it sits directly under your face, the collar is the focal point of any shirt, and of any tailored ensemble. There are five basic styles: button down, club, tab, point, and spread. While each possesses its own unique charm, not all are appropriate on all men. For some collars flatter certain shapes while others offend them, and a man must take into account the shape of his face when selecting one. As Flusser has written, "Think of your face as a portrait and your shirt collar as its frame." Just as it would be unreasonable to cram *The Night Watch* into a frame made for *Self Portrait in a Cap*, so do wide faces look like bowling balls atop small collars, narrow faces like golf balls on big collars; and long necks look stork-like in low collars, while short necks disappear in high collars. Custom shirtmakers—whether made-to-measure or bespoke—cut their collars to frame the face, but ready-to-wear manufacturers make theirs too low and too small. To see this, look no further than Tim Russert, host of *Meet the Press,* whose collars are much too small and their points much too short for his face. He would look infinitely better in a collar with four inch points; conversely, only a pinhead requires collar points shorter than two and three-quarter inches.

The collar also determines a shirt's level of formality. Informal ones can dress down dressy suits, while formal collars can smarten up more casual attire. The best dressers always identify at least one formal and one informal collar flattering to their face and buy many examples of each. The least formal—and the only dress shirt collar that can be worn without a tie—is the button down, a soft, unlined collar whose points button to the shirt-front. The best have points long enough to effect a "roll," a gentle, purposeful curve that accentuates the collar's inherent casualness. Italian dandies wear theirs unbuttoned, which looks even more casual but somewhat sloppy; and to forgo willingly the insouciant beauty of the roll is a practice best left to those with style to burn. Though reputedly invented by English polo players who tired of their shirt collars flapping in their faces, the button down has long been a staple of American dress. The once-august firm of Brooks Brothers was responsible for vaulting it to international popularity. After the Second World War, it became—along with the Sack suit and cordovan shoes—a required element of the American Ivy League uniform. The button down goes especially well with sports jackets, from informal tweeds to worsted blazers, and also lowers the formality of suits; but it is too informal to wear with dressy ties or anything double-breasted. It should also be avoided by those ample of neck and rotund in face, because its soft folds only amplify those inherent in the wearer.

The club, or rounded, collar—not the shifty sharkfin collars of Pat Riley but the barbershop quartet collars of Ross Perot—is the most antique looking of all collars, owing to its resemblance to the stiff, detachable collars that were ubiquitous in the years before the First World War. Neither formal nor informal, too costumey to be worn for business, too fussy for sportswear, it looks fine on slim, square faces, but accentuates the roundness of round ones.

The more open its front and the more swept back its points, the better it looks. Straighter versions look best soft and either tabbed or pinned, for this distinguishes them from their stiff, starched ancestor.

The tab collar is another innovation of the duke of Windsor. Its tab consists of two small strips of cloth that attach behind the tie knot and pull the collar points together, fixing the knot in place and creating a graceful arch to the tie. On ready-made examples the tab will attach via a snap or button, but bespoke shirtmakers still make them with two loops held together by a brass stud. Dressy enough for a dark suit and casual enough for an unconstructed summer jacket, the tab is the most versatile of all collars. Noted dandy Tom Wolfe wears none but these, cut as high as his chin and starched into submission, to complement his long neck and antique-looking clothes. But men with shorter necks or narrow faces are better off with a soft version, worn without stays. Bulky ties and large knots cause tab collars to bunch inelegantly, as can be seen on Donald Rumsfeld.

The other two collars are at root the same, the only difference being their degree of spread. And truly there are as many such collars as there are points on a protractor. But to simplify matters, I say that point collars are all those whose opening angle is less than 90 degrees, and spread collars those whose opening is greater. Widest of all is the cutaway, which can be as open as 180 degrees. It is sometimes called the Windsor collar, after the duke, who designed it to accommodate his large tie knots. This is the most dandified and formal of all collars, too formal for anything but suits, or perhaps a double-breasted blazer; indeed, it looks especially smart with double-breasted jackets. It most flatters those with thin or long faces; meatheads should avoid them. But the longest and leanest faces should also avoid them, because the vertical line of the face combined with the near-horizontal line of the cutaway looks like an upside-down T. They should choose instead a spread collar whose opening is no greater than 130 degrees. Favored by Charles, prince of Wales, these are more common, less striking, and not so formal that they cannot be worn with a blazer.

The point is the most staid of collars, favored by the old and flattering to those with excessively round faces; its narrowness harms those with long necks or faces. And, just as extremely narrow faces should not be paired with extreme cutaways, so should extremely wide faces not be paired with point collars whose opening is less than 60 degrees. Whatever the shape of your face, point collars so closed they look as though borrowed from the cast of *Goodfellas* must be shunned. In our time, the point collar is seen every day on George Bush. It takes well to pinning, and dandies will only wear it thus.

Cuffs are the other factor that determines a shirt's level of formality. There are two kinds, button (or "barrel") and French. ("Cocktail" or "Bond" cuffs, a clumsy attempt to combine the two, are too pretentious to be elegant.) The former, more common by far, is a round cuff that fastens via a button; or, in the case of some shirtmakers, two or even three. It is appropriate with any collar save the cutaway but dresses down the more formal ones. The more formal, more dandified French cuff is a flat panel of cloth that folds back over itself—hence the English term "double cuff," which the French resent as evidence of Francophobia—and requires cufflinks to fasten. It is never appropriate with a button down collar; some shirtmakers believe that it is appropriate only with the spread, but I have seen tab-collared shirts with French cuffs that looked smart. French cuff shirts should always be made of fine cloth and discreet patterns; rougher weaves like oxford and jazzy, large-scale patterns are too informal. And they should be worn only with suits, and only those of worsted or flannel. A most dandified touch is to have a colored or patterned French cuff shirt made with a white collar. An echo of the days when collars were separate from shirts, these became unpopular in the middle of the last century when they became a favored mode of mafiosi. They were revived in the 1980s by captains of industry and Wall Street tycoons and in our time have come to be seen as symbols of plutocracy. Yet their true origin is in WASPish thrift. Because the plutocrats of old did not like to buy new clothes, when the collars and cuffs of their shirts frayed beyond what could be considered quaint, they would replace them with white if the original cloth could not be found. Because these resembled the detachable collars *de rigueur* for so long during the 19th and early 20th centuries, they were readily accepted. Contrast works best with formal collars like the spread; on button downs never. Many uncouth shirtmakers will make contrast collars or cuffs or both with a stripe or decoration of some kind, a vulgarity favored by the ostentatious and especially popular in Southern Italy and the Middle East. Indeed, the practice originated with bespoke shirtmakers from Beirut—a city which, when Lebanon was democratic and peaceful, supported a thriving bespoke clothing trade. And they took the practice with them to Europe and America when the Syrians conquered and ruined their country. But gentlemen will not wear them, and know that the color of a contrast collar must always be white, and its cuffs must be French, though these may either be white or "self" (the same cloth as the body of the garment).

No matter what its collar or cuff mode, all dress shirts should fit alike. The neck should look, but not feel, snug. You should be able to turn your head comfortably and pull your tie firmly up into the collar without sensing strangulation. If your collar gapes or stands away from the neck at any point, it is too large. If you feel compelled to unbutton it or loosen your tie, it is too small: well-fitting collars can be worn all day with the tie pulled up and cause no discomfort. When the cuffs are unbuttoned, they should cover a third of your hand; when buttoned, they should rest at the base of your thumb with the excess sleeve length gathering above; thus can you move and bend your arms without the sleeves riding up your forearm, and you will always show shirt cuff beneath your jacket sleeves. Some shirtmakers dispute this, saying that if the pattern is drawn correctly—with a small armhole, the proper taper and pitch to the sleeve, and the right bend at the elbow— then the sleeves can be cut exactly as long as your arm and they will never ride up. But few know how to do this, and many others believe that the gather above the cuff is aesthetically pleasing; so with most shirtmakers it is safer to ask for longer sleeves. A shirt's body should have a definite waist and be long enough to cover your seat; otherwise it will not stay tucked in. And it may be cut full or slim. In our country, the slim shirt is only available from European designers or else bespoke. For since ready-made shirts are sized only according to collar and sleeve, they must be able to fit the ample as readily as the slender, and this is possible only with tent-like dimensions. Americans prefer full-cut shirts, some say because we are fat, or do not trust ourselves to avoid becoming fat, but I believe it is owing more to our having little experience with bespoke shirts. The French and many Italians favor tapered shirts—with the Romans and Milanese wearing shirts that fit almost like gloves—while the English prefer shirts with a bit more room, and the Neapolitans like theirs small in the shoulders but blousy in the sleeves and around the middle. Dandies of all nations wear their shirts slim enough so that no excess cloth bunches up around the waist when standing, but full enough to cause no discomfort when sitting.

A shirt's quality is judged in two modes: how fine is its cloth and how well it is made. Whereas all bespoke shirtmakers once sewed their shirts largely by hand, in our time only the Neapolitans and a handful of others in Italy and France uphold this art. Its partisans claim that, over time, the hand-sewn armhole, yoke (where the back meets the shoulders), and collar band seams help the shirt conform to the wearer's body, providing better fit and greater comfort. The shoulders of Neapolitan shirts are hand-shirred with small pleats whose extra fullness is intended to provide greater comfort and freedom of movement. Yet handmade buttonholes, while infinitely more beautiful than machine made, are exponentially more expensive and purely decorative. All the London and New York shirtmakers, and even some of the Romans and the Milanese, stitch their shirts by machine. The best ones use only single-needle construction, in which each seam is sewn twice with the same needle—once on the top or outside, once on the inside—producing a single row of minute stitches that is smooth as glass and tight as a drum. Two rows of stitching on each seam—called double-needle construction—is faster and easier to make but less durable, because both rows together are weaker than one single needle seam, and less attractive, because the cloth in between rows will pucker after washing, and because fewer seams look better than more.

Beyond stitching, well-made shirts share certain other qualities. Most dandies believe that, when buttoned, the collar should form a perfect inverted V above the tie knot. But those who favor large tie knots, like the duke of Windsor and the Neapolitans, recognize that a smidgen of tie space helps the knot fit under the collar without causing its points to lift; and the narrower a collar's spread, the more space is needed. Button downs always look better with a half-inch of tie space. No matter the collar style, not so much as a millimeter of collar band should ever be visible above the tie knot. The collars of *Wall Street Week* host Geoff Colvin, a well-dressed man in other respects, never come together to form a V and always show collar band. Collars should also completely cover the band at the sides and around through the back; no seam should be visible peeking out from under. Some have written that a yoke (the cloth that covers the shoulders) made from two pieces rather than one is a sure sign of a quality shirt. And they are correct, in that a split yoke takes longer and is more difficult to make. But its only function is to allow bespoke shirtmakers to accommodate differing left and right shoulder slopes and measurements; on ready-to-wear shirts they serve no purpose, apart from allowing stripes and checks to be chevroned (or angled) at the yoke, something all bespoke shirtmakers should do, because it looks dashing. Better manufacturers include a small pleat over each shoulder blade; these serve the same purpose as the fullness over the blades of a drape-cut jacket. Bespoke shirtmakers can incorporate this fullness without pleats, but unless such shirts are ironed by hand, the yoke seam will look sloppy. Slim-bodied Italian and French shirts often lack both pleats and fullness, whereas American shirts tend to have ugly and useless box pleats—two pleats about an inch apart over the spine. There should also be two or three small pleats where the cuff attaches to the sleeve; on cheap shirts the excess sleeve cloth will be crammed haphazardly into the cuff. The sleeve gauntlet should close via a small button and horizontal buttonhole (to match the direction of the buttonholes on the cuffs), and all buttons on well-made shirts should be mother-of-pearl. These always look and feel better than plastic, and the finest—cut from thick oyster shells—are also more durable. On shirts made from striped or checked cloth, the patterns should match exactly at the gauntlets, where the sleeves meet the yoke, and at the pocket (though dandies prefer the cleaner, more elegant look of pocketless shirts).

Turning then to cloth, I say that all good shirts are made of cotton. For, as with all clothing, synthetic fabrics are an abomination, but especially for shirts, which sit next to the skin; for besides looking cheap, synthetics scratch and irritate the skin, whereas cotton caresses it. The best cottons are grown in Egypt and the Caribbean and woven in Switzerland and Italy; fine cotton used to be grown in the American Southeast, on the islands off the Georgia coast, but today Sea Island is a brand name owned by cotton growers in the West Indies. Silk, a favorite of gangsters and sheikhs, should be avoided because it is hard to clean, has a gaudy sheen, is too hot, and the best cottons today can meet and exceed its smoothness and luster. Linen makes a cool and breathable summer shirt, but unless it is shrunk before it is cut it will have to be dry-cleaned at vexing expense, and few makers bother or know how to shrink linen properly. Some men also find it stiff and scratchy; and it is so wrinkly that even ordinary cotton performs like 20-ounce tweed by comparison. But linen-cotton blends combine the virtues of linen with the convenience of cotton. Like suitings, the quality of shirtings varies widely. The thinner the individual yarns, the higher the yarn number of the cloth; and the higher its yarn number, the silkier a cloth will feel, the more lustrous it will look, and the more it will cost. Yarn numbers range from the ordinary 30s found in cheap department stores to the more common 80s used by better ready-to-wear makers to the rare and frightfully expensive 200s. Yet, as in the case of suitings, thin yarns are but one indicator of quality. Long staple 140s woven on slow looms that neither stretch nor break the fibers are a better value than some of the 170s rushed to market off high-speed looms. All the best shirtings are two-by-two.

In general, the smoother the cloth, the more formal the shirt. Smooth, tight broadcloth—with its lovely, natural sheen that displays colors and patterns to great advantage—is the most formal. Slightly less formal is end-on-end, a weave of alternating lighter and darker colored threads that produces a check so minute it looks solid from a distance but textured up close, though in truth it is neither. Twill weaves, with their diagonal ribbing, are heavier and denser than broadcloth and make good shirts for cool weather. Poplin is a broadcloth that looks like a twill but is denser and harder, for the weft yarns are thicker than the warp. Oxford is a textured weave made chiefly in three modes: regular, pinpoint, and royal. The first two are tiny bird's-eye patterns, different only in scale, yet large enough to be too informal for any collar but the button down (though pinpoint in small checks might take a moderate spread). Royal oxford, a rich-looking minute diamond weave, is the rare shirting that takes equally well to button downs ands spreads and all collars in between. Because of their thickness, oxfords make fine winter shirts but are too hot for summer. Voile and batiste—favorites of the Southern Italians—are thin, airy weaves that make wonderful summer shirts, but their translucence shows every chest hair. Some shirtmakers attempt to obviate this by using two layers, but double-voile is warmer than single, and wearing any but the thinnest undershirt with single-voile shirts similarly defeats their cooling properties. These are the essential weaves; some others are also useful, such as self-herringbones for wear with suits and brushed-cotton "flannelette" with tweeds. Though expensive and prevalent in the swatch books of the great bespoke shirtmaking houses, jacquards—cloths with raised stripes, dots, and other repeating woven patterns—only look good in patterns of two or more colors, and even then rarely. White-on-white versions are best left to loan sharks and lounge singers.

Though color and pattern are the twin pillars of shirtings, all men must own several solid whites; for if solids are the foundation of a man's shirt wardrobe, then solid white is the cornerstone. It is the most formal of colors—indeed, in broadcloth, it is the most formal of all shirts—and it is safe with every garment from worsteds to tweeds, with colors from midnight blue to cream, with all varieties of necktie, and for every situation, because it is never offensive or dandified and allows you to disappear into a crowd should the need arise. Its virtues are that it is the perfect backdrop for brilliant and shiny, dressy and dandified ties; and it provides a neutral ground between a busily patterned jacket and complex tie, especially if their color schemes are wholly different.

But dandies have always preferred colored shirts, and have several solids in various hues. The most useful is blue, for it is not so jaunty as pink or yellow, yet not so severe as white; it warms light complexions and cools dark ones; and is most versatile, complementing jackets and ties of all colors. Pink is underutilized by most men, who fear its effeminate connotations, but dandies know it is a smart accompaniment to a wide range of suitings—particularly gray, which it elevates from banker drab to the summit of style—and a marvelous background for a wide variety of ties, especially summer's bold and colorful neckwear. Other useful colors include yellow, the preppy hue par excellence, which works best in oxford button downs and with browns and tweeds; faint gray, a favorite among the great dressers of the 1930s; cream, a more lively alternative to white; rare and dandified lavender; and the still-rarer sage green. If there are rules one could give for solid-colored shirts, they are these: their color should harmonize with jacket and tie or else be offensive to neither; they are appropriate only in the colors mentioned above, and only in soft, subtle, shades—always lighter than the jacket worn therewith. The only exception might be a French blue shirt with a tan, cream, or light gray suit; but even this fine color is often worn in too dark a shade. Under no circumstances can you wear those faddish, gangster-looking solids found so often in department stores: candy-apple red, electric blue, forest green, Inca gold, and the like. Whatever designers or salesmen say, these are not dress shirts but casual wear, and even then belong only at craps tables.

But by far the worst and most tasteless abomination one can commit is to wear a black shirt with a tie. Nonetheless, one sees many men who not only wear them, but compound the disaster by wearing light jackets and white ties. Unless you are cast as Nathan Detroit, this is the surest path to sartorial damnation.

But lest indignation cloud our minds, let us turn to pattern. Here the possibilities expand infinitely, for certain colors—like red, green, peach, and purple—that are unacceptable for solids work wonderfully in patterns. Stripes are the most common pattern and the one even timid men can occasionally bring themselves to try. Striped shirts vary according to the color of their ground and the color, gauge, complexity, and frequency of the stripes. The most common ground is white; a colored ground with a white stripe is more dandified, and with a colored stripe, more dandified still. Stripes range in thickness from bold bengals to minute hairlines. And truly the types and variations of stripes are infinite—from shadow to antique to double- and triple- and four-bar to many that do not have names; and to describe them all would be tiresome. But, generally, the more intricate and colorful the stripes, the more dandified the shirt, but the harder it is to mate with jackets and ties. Supremely dandified are horizontal stripes, a favorite mode of classic times that was revived for the film *Wall Street*. Its boldness strikes terror into the hearts of most men, especially investment bankers, who fear being dismissed by their colleagues as "Gekko wannabes." Whatever the type or gauge of stripes, the thicker and farther apart they are, the less formal the shirt. No man looks good in stripes separated by more than a half inch of ground.

Checks, which offer even more possibilities than stripes, differ according to their scale and complexity. The largest in scale are appropriate only for casual wear. For dress shirts, three checks have gained widespread acceptance: miniature windowpane, in which all of the stripes that make up the check are of the same color; tattersall, in which the stripes are of two colors (blue and black and red and black being the most common); and gingham, which looks like a tablecloth in a cheap Italian restaurant, but slightly more refined. But there are many other checks besides these—fancier, more complex, and more lively, many of them unique to one mill, and sold only to bespoke shirtmakers; and some of these have bolt after bolt of unique cloth piled high in every corner of the store, made decades before and never to be made again. This is one of the many reasons why all well-dressed men—even those whom off-the-rack shirts fit perfectly—have their shirts bespoke.

The male cast of *60 Minutes*—except Steve Kroft, who dresses like a Nordstrom salesman—shows what effects shirtings can have on the wardrobe. Mike Wallace always looks good but never smart because he always wears a blue button down. And though blue goes well with his ubiquitous tan suit and dark tie, he could learn from Charlie Rose not to wear large tie knots with small collars, and from Ed Bradley and Morley Safer that diversity in shirtings confers greater style. Bradley's shirts fit perfectly, and mostly look rakish. He is a great wearer of solids of all colors and shades (although he occasionally wears some that give me pause), and also loves stripes and wears them to great effect, outdoing virtually everyone else in network news, who, despite the obvious expense of their clothes, tend to look dull. But Morley Safer is the greatest wearer of shirts in our time. He is enamored of checks and wears only unique and unusual varieties thereof, which re-dound to his glory. And he loves them so much that one never sees him in a boring solid or stripe. He alone keeps the checked-shirt alive in this country (for it has not fallen into such neglect in Europe, and especially England, where checked shirts are almost a religion), but his example has yet to inspire widespread imitation. But I do not blame him, but rather the decrepit state of American tastes, discussed at length below.

So let a man acquire and wear a plethora of patterned shirts of all scales and colors, enough to make Daisy Buchanan cry: he will always be praised for his prudence and style. For the many are captive to white and blue and cannot see beyond them, and since they always wear blue and gray suits, they always look the same. Thus he who wears striped and checked shirts can distinguish himself from them, even if he wears those same two suits for weeks. A certain politician of our time, whom it is not well to name, never wears anything but striped and checked shirts and yet is always reëlected. If he wore only white and blue shirts, he would not be remembered, and his office would have been taken from him long ago.

XIX.

Of the Difference Between
Formality and Dandification

B ut because I have spoken of the most important of the garments mentioned above, I want to discourse on some important matters briefly under this generality, that a man,
when putting together ensembles, should think about how formal
are his garments and how dandified. When he understands this, he
will have done his part and will find no difficulty in dressing with
style and grace.

What makes for dandification is panache or strikingness combined with rarity. While often unusual, the dandified always follows the classic rules of dress, or else is based on a judicious
breaking of those rules. It is never costume—not spats and ascots,
but vests and handkerchiefs. Yet there is always some risk in wear-

ing what is dandified, unless you have so much reputation that a certain eccentricity, even extravagance, is taken to be your due. Formality is dressiness; or, to say better, solemnity combined with obeisance to established modes of propriety, especially those concerning occasions held to be grave and important. If ever you are at a loss as to whether this or that garment is formal or not, you should consider how you would feel wearing it to your mother's funeral. Heads of state, captains of industry, and those subject to the whims of large numbers of people tend at all times to dress formally. There is no risk in wearing what is formal, unless you wear it to the beach or an amusement park or some similar place. That these two principles are in tension was taught covertly by Wodehouse, who represented formality in the character of Jeeves and dandification in Bertie Wooster. There is hardly a story about them in which Bertie's enthusiasm for some adventurous garment does not run afoul of Jeeves's stern sense of propriety. To show two sartorially knowledgeable gentlemen continually disputing the virtue of various clothing means nothing other than that a man needs to know how to use both principles; and the one without the other is not elegant.

Dandification and especially formality exist along continuums. And while we may say confidently of the easy cases that this or that garment is more or less formal or dandified than some other (for example, a tweed jacket is less formal than a worsted suit and white suitings are more dandified than gray), the closer two garments are on the continuum, the harder these judgments are to make. Is a two-piece double-breasted suit more or less formal than a single-breasted with peaked lapels and double-breasted vest? Is dark brown more or less dandified than light gray? All we can know is that certain characteristics like darkness and smoothness generally make garments more formal and their opposites make them more dandified. Most every garment is appropriate within a range along the formality continuum. Thus ginger suede monk straps complement a tweed jacket at the lower end and a worsted suit at the upper end but are too dressy for streetwear and not dressy enough for black tie. But there is much overlap between various garments; so that, for instance, a blue button down and an antique stripe spread collar will go with many of the same suits, but the button down reaches further down into the formality scale and the spread collar further up. Also, the further apart two garments are on the formality scale, the less appropriate is wearing them together, and thus the more dandified. Thus suede loafers and a sock tie worn with a midnight blue business suit would be wrong in a boardroom but perhaps suave in a Via Veneto café. But combining many garments of the same or similar levels of formality is always safe. The opposite is true of dandification. Dandified items should be kept to a minimum lest too much plumage turn you into a peacock. Besides, striking garments achieve their greatest effect in subdued surroundings.

But let that suffice as to general reasoning. And because I do not know how to discourse on this matter further except through examples, I say that, short of evening dress, the most formal combination a man can wear—what Tom Wolfe calls "sartorial armor"—is a navy suit, white shirt, dark tie, and black shoes, and that none of these is the least bit dandified. Also formal are solid suits, and solids generally, and dark colors—except in the case of shirts and handkerchiefs, where white is the most formal because, these things dwelling close to the skin, they have more occasion to become soiled, and in the days before cleaning was cheap and easy, white was a mark of gentility. Conversely, white suits and shoes are informal to the highest degree but dandified to the highest degree—as are suede shoes, and Panama hats, and tab collar shirts. Yet, in all other cases, color is more dandified than its absence, but rarely more formal, except for dark blue suits, as was said. Similarly, patterns are always more dandified than solids but rarely more formal.

Textures are usually more dandified than smooth fabrics, and also less formal, because most have long been associated with the country, where men have always dressed with more flair and less sobriety than in town. And this is why a solid knit tie is at once more dandified and less formal than a solid satin tie of the same color, and why the same is true of suede shoes as opposed to calf, and also of Saxony or gabardine or Cheviot suits as opposed to plain worsteds. So too are cotton and linen suitings more dandified than tropical worsteds, because they so conspicuously wrinkle.

And just as there are some things which are neither formal nor dandified—like single-breasted blazers, button down shirts, and penny loafers (for nothing common can be dandified)—so too are there some which are both, such as the double-breasted jacket. Thus it has always been a favorite of the best dressed, such as the duke of Windsor, Dean Acheson, and Fred Astaire. But the greatest of all wearers of them was Douglas Fairbanks, Jr. Toward the end of his life, one saw him on the American Movie Classics channel, before it became hip, discussing the Golden Age of cinema and always smartly attired in bespoke double-breasted suits, some of which were made more than three decades before and yet still looked rakish. And you can still see him in his many movies wearing wondrously tailored double-breasteds, with appropriately formal spread-collar shirts and grenadine ties. And when you see him you will understand the necessity of having at least one double-breasted garment in your wardrobe, for the most formal and jubilant occasions.

In addition, some things, though not dandified in themselves, are made dandified by their usage. Fred Astaire loved the soft nonchalance of Brooks Brothers button down shirts and knew that this least dandified of garments became so when paired with a three-piece suit. Similarly, he always preferred brown shoes, because of their added color and richness, to black, even when wearing nothing else that was brown. And he often used solid ties, so grave in themselves, to balance and unify a shirt and jacket of differing lively patterns. Some have said that he occasionally took this mode too far, as when he wore six-on-one double-breasted suits with button down shirts. But he never went so far as to wear moccasins with a three-piece suit, or an antique-stripe contrast collar shirt with a blazer and khakis. For, as was said above, not through haphazard mixing but by creating slight incongruities he became the foremost dandy of his age and maintained himself in that place with many spirited and daring innovations. Yet one cannot call it virtue to juxtapose the soft roll of a button down collar with the precise angles of double-breasted lapels; such modes can enable one to acquire notoriety, but not glory. Still, if one considers the virtue of Astaire in creating ensembles for himself and styles for the whole world, one does not see why he has to be judged inferior to any most excellent dresser. Nonetheless, his reckless disregard of established modes, together with the glee he took in flaunting them, do not permit him to be celebrated among the most fastidious of men.

I wish to consider this matter further. Many have observed that the clothing and habits of men vary by their province or occupation. It would be too long and exalted a matter to describe fully even the few most famous and stylish. But, to give some flavor of what I mean, it is known that the English favor double-breasted suits, bold stripes, and black cap-toes for a look of crisp formality in town; and tweed suits, tattersall shirts, wool challis ties, and brown suede brogues in the country. Museum curators and partners in white shoe law firms and investment banks prefer expensive clothes in solid colors—"subdued and rich, as only these bastards know how to do it"—a look exemplified by Kofi Annan, or Michael Douglas in *The Game*. American college students, especially the WASPs, were once famous for their tweed jackets, gray flannel trousers, button down shirts, and cordovan loafers; and when they grew up they graduated to Sack suits, wing tips, and repp ties—a look exemplified by William F. Buckley, Jr., who, though not a WASP, for many years played one on television. No American college student has worn anything so formal as a collared shirt since 1965, but the Japanese have adopted this look, dubbing it "trad"—a name that crossed the Pacific to be adopted by some Americans. Italians from Rome to the south love bold patterns and bright colors; and while the Romans favor close-fitting clothes, the Neapolitans prefer theirs fuller, with more drape. Lawyers love Hermès ties, investment bankers suspenders, and college professors bow ties. All of these, and many others, are almost uniforms for those who adhere to them. But you should eschew uniforms and instead do as the Milanese do, and wear elements of one and another uniform together. For they understand that the twin capitals of male elegance are London and Naples: the former for cool weather and honored traditions, the latter for warm temperatures and tasteful innovation. And blessed with an economy similar to London's, a culture akin to Naples, and a climate that varies to replicate the former's fog and the latter's heat, the men of Milan are able to take without hesitation whatever looks good from both cities and make it their own. Thus will you see them wearing flannels and tweeds in the winter and quarter-lined frescos, linens, and mohairs in the summer; and somber blues and grays for business, and light colors and bold patterns for leisure. And they take from all good traditions and freely mix things together. They always wear brown shoes, even with dark blue suits; and in their boldness they will pair a Brooks Brothers button down with a worsted suit and Macclesfield tie, a favorite mode of famed dandy Gianni Agnelli. Milanese designer Luciano Barbera exemplifies their spirit, taking tweeds from the English, button downs from the Americans, and silk foulards from the French, making a new whole from the various parts. All but the best-dressed Englishmen look as though they are following to the letter the dictates of a rulebook. But the best-dressed Italian not only looks better but also as if he came up with his style entirely on his own.

One might give infinite other examples of this matter, some touching on model, some on color, some on fabric, and some on pattern, but all united by the juxtaposition of the showy and the sober. I conclude, therefore, that the stylish dresser varies the modes of his clothing; and, while avoiding modes which should not exist at all, he judiciously mixes models, colors, and patterns to effect a less studied and more nonchalant look.

It might perhaps appear to many, considering the sartorial habits of some American president, that these modes are not natural to our countrymen and so it is folly for us to imitate them. Since I want to respond to this objection, I shall discuss the habits of certain presidents, showing that in many cases they dressed better than you think. And I want it to suffice for me to take all the modern presidents, from Franklin Roosevelt to the younger Bush: these were Roosevelt, Harry Truman, Dwight Eisenhower, John Kennedy, Lyndon Johnson, Richard Nixon, Gerald Ford, Jimmy Carter, Ronald Reagan, George Bush and his son, and Bill Clinton. And first it has to be considered that whereas heads of state in other countries have leave to dress well, either because their position does not depend upon the people, or else because their people are not offended by fine clothes, American presidents must contend with a people that demands formality from their leaders but eschews and punishes dandification.

For the cause mentioned above, Eisenhower was rewarded with a second term, for he always dressed formally, but never with panache (for vests and hats, while dandified today, were common in his time). Ford almost won despite the corruption of his predecessor, because his formal yet unassuming clothes gave him credit with the people in sartorially troubled times. Though he had no choice but to wear wide ties, big collars, and wide lapels—for none but these were made or sold during his administration—he always chose the least oversized and most sedate.

When he was leader of the Senate, Johnson dressed garishly, in the worst traditions of his home state. But when he ran for national office he was forced to dress modestly, and his few forays into dandification, such as cowboy boots, were consistent with his roots. Later he became envious of the fine clothes he saw on Kennedy, and sought out a London tailor whom he told to make him "look like a British diplomat." Thereafter he began to dress again with more flair—in side vents, slanted pockets, bold stripes, and the like—and, losing credit with the people, he was ruined. Nixon, who famously wore black wing tips to the beach, never lacked formality, but somehow became enthralled by those gaudy ties and fishmouth lapels that came into vogue in the 1970s. He would have been ruined regardless, but in wearing these he did not help himself. For while they might have been popular with a few, none of these voted for him; and even they did not want to see such clothes on their president, whom they expected to uphold the dignity of his office. Later, when he wanted to rehabilitate his reputation, he returned to the plain style that had served him well before he became president, and this helped him establish himself as an elder statesman.

The first George Bush dressed formally, and—he thought—not at all dandified. Yet the people recognized in all those repp ties, Sack suits, and linen hankies the quality known as preppyness. Because this reminded them of his patrician heritage, it fixed in their mind the impression that he did not understand or care about them, and so he was ruined. His son, learning from this error, dresses with the crisp formality of a CEO, but without any hint of preppyness, so that if he is ruined, it will not be because of his clothes.

Reviewing now, by contrast, the habits of Roosevelt, Kennedy, and Reagan, you will find them very formal but also somewhat dandified. To satisfy the people, they always dressed with the dignity required of a president; yet to satisfy themselves, they allowed subtle professions of style; and all except Kennedy were reëlected. Reagan grew accustomed to fine clothing during his days in Hollywood, and when he became president he did not want to give it up. His great virtue enabled him to arrange his ensembles so that while the cut of his suits was a bit sharp, they were first-rate in quality and fit, and the whole always formal and proper. Fortune provided him nothing but the opportunity to follow a president who had offended the people by dressing shoddily, so that his stylishness was welcome to them. And remembering that he had been a movie star, they could even tolerate in him some measure of dandification. Kennedy always dressed with style, and when he ventured into dandification—for instance wearing a top hat to his inauguration—the people not only forgave him but loved him more, because they judged the occasion worthy, and because he looked smart in it. And even when, in the conduct of his day-to-day affairs, he avoided overt dandification, he was always better dressed than everyone around him, partly because of his huge collection of shoes (which hardly anyone but himself noticed), partly because after acquiring a taste for the Drape while a student in London in the 1930s, he never abandoned it—not in the 1950s, when every upper-class American was wearing the Sack, nor in the 1960s, when the Continental was sweeping the *haut monde*. Instead he had it subtly modified by his American tailor to look less dramatically British and more home-grown. Dozens of American manufacturers, and millions of American men, tried with varying success to copy his look, and thus was born the minimally padded, moderately shaped two-button suit that is ubiquitous even now in American stores and on American streets. Roosevelt dressed like a Hudson River Valley grandee, and since he was one, offended no one—not even at Yalta, where he wore a black velvet cape lined in scarlet satin. For because Democrats are held to be more sympathetic to the people and less priggish, and also because it is considered rarer for a tribune of the people to dress with style, they are given more leeway. Whereas Republicans, who are held to be not only avatars of business and the rich but also scolds, give offense if they do not dress formally yet plainly; thus was Nixon able to save his career by mentioning his wife's cloth coat. For these reasons, dandification that is condemned as insolence in a Republican is praised as elegance in a Democrat, provided he is wellborn. Thus could Roosevelt dress in any manner he pleased and not be hurt by it, whereas had Landon or Willkie or Dewey attained the office and tried the same, they would have been ruined.

But let us come to Truman, who was the least formal and most dandified of presidents. He was the only modern president to wear bow ties, and until recently the only one to wear double-breasted suits. He also favored fancy hats—Panamas and snap brims and such—and did not hesitate to wear lively patterns, light colors, two-tone shoes, and wrinkly cloths such as linen and cotton. And he always wore a pocket handkerchief. Oftentimes in photos you will see him gathered with his advisors, who all blend together in their plain, dark, single-breasted suits and white shirts, while he stands out in his boldly checked double-breasted suit and striped shirt. And doubtless the delight he took in dressing stemmed from his days as a haberdasher. But eventually his informality, which at first had seemed so endearing, came to grate on the people. He tried to assuage their anger by switching to dark three-piece suits, but he was too late, and to avoid ruin he chose not to run again.

It remains now to tell the habits of Clinton. And because these were notable, I want to show briefly how well he judged necessity in choosing his wardrobe. When Clinton first sought the office, knowing of the weakness of his rivals, he did not take steps to change his mode of dress, which had been bedraggled since he first put on clothes. But when a scare was put into him in New Hampshire, he judged that what had worked in Arkansas might not avail him nationwide. So he adopted the Washington uniform of a dark blue suit, white shirt, and red tie, and was soon for the first time being called presidential. And he became president. Then, having gained a taste for the high life, he began to find ordinary clothes intolerable. His Hollywood friends introduced him to the designer Donna Karan, who soon began supplying all his clothes. But when the Congress was lost to him, throwing his administration into disarray, an advisor warned him that to regain credit with the people, he had to return to modest modes of dress. Thus was he reëlected. And though he wished immediately to return to his former ostentation, scandal forced him to remain unobtrusive for many months, though when he traveled abroad, he allowed himself more panache. Once he judged that his enemies were unable to hurt him with the scandal, he began to dress with more display than ever, and became the first president since Truman to wear double-breasted suits. Later, when a new and more dangerous scandal threatened to ruin him, he returned to modesty, even resorting to the sobriety of the Washington uniform when addressing the people about the scandal. Yet he and his allies were so successful at deflecting the people's anger from himself and onto his enemies that these lost an election that all the wise of our time judged them fated to win. With his enemies in disarray, he again returned to opulence. And though the people never believed him, he was able to finish his term because his infinite cleverness made him so admirable to his allies and acceptable to the people that the latter remained somehow astonished and stupefied, while the former were reverent and satisfied. Thus whoever examines minutely the habits of this man will find him a most astute judge of the mood of the people and his own exposure to danger, and will see that he varied his dress accordingly, and will not marvel that he was able to escape ruin on so many occasions.

I do not want to reason about Carter, who, because he dressed altogether contemptibly, was quickly ruined—except to say that it is one thing to wear Hawaiian shirts in Key West or jeans and cowboy boots when splitting wood, and another to address the people from the Oval Office in a sweater. But, coming to the conclusion of this discourse, I say that those in our time whose positions depend on the people are forced when they dress to take account of their humors; and that politicians are hurt both by a lack of formality and too much dandification, but entertainers and others must take care to include some dandification, as was said.

But let us return to our matter. I say that whoever considers the discourse written above will see that formality and dandification are the twin factors that determine which combinations look good, which shoddy, which inappropriate, and which ridiculous. For each individual garment is formal or informal to its own degree, and also dandified or plain; and through judicious mixing you can combine the two qualities, or their absence, to produce ensembles that are themselves either formal or informal, dandified or somber, or some degree in between. In all cases you must avoid the extremes of the one or the other. Therefore, a man cannot follow the predilections of Jeeves, lest he end up looking like an undertaker, nor can he in all things imitate Wooster without coming off like a riverboat gambler; but he should take from Jeeves as much formality as the occasion requires, and from Wooster as much dandification as it allows.

XX.

When and How a Dandy Should Wear Odd Jackets and Trousers to Be Held in Esteem

Nothing makes a dandy so esteemed as to be able to combine odd jackets and trousers elegantly. Also called sports jackets, because of their origin as garments worn for play, odd jackets are those made without matching trousers. In our time such disparate ensembles are less formal than the matching suit, whereas until about the First World War, suits were considered sports clothes and more formal attire took odd trousers. That principle stretched back to the silk hose worn at royal courts, which matched neither coat nor vest. The French Revolution eliminated its adherents, at least in France, and made it unpopular among the *incroyables* and other utopian anti-monarchists, who began to wear English riding breeches, which were considered more democratic. Yet these too did not match; as very rarely do even the boldest innovators dare to introduce anything altogether new. When the frock coat emerged as the business coat of 19th century it also took odd trousers, as did the morning coat and the stroller. The odd jacket as we know it emerged from the warmer colonies of the British Empire, where men could not bear to play cricket or row sculls in tweed suits. So they had coats made from local cloth, such as cotton madras in India, and wore them—contrary to custom—with the trousers of their lightest doeskin suits. In America, this look became popular with the resort-bound upper class, who took to wearing their blue serge suit coats with white flannel trousers. After the lounge suit took the frock coat's place as standard business wear, matching clothes were suddenly more formal than odd ensembles (the sole exception being day-time formal wear) and odd jackets and trousers came to dominate not just resort wear but all non-business occasions. And it often happens that some innovation is introduced for a reason that is later forgotten or abandoned but the style remains as a rule. Thus the canon of rules is filled with contradictions and confusions.

But, returning to the clothes, I say that great care must be taken in pairing odd jackets with trousers so as to produce a combination that not only does not offend but pleases. In our time, few have mastered this art. For with the rise of "business casual," men have fewer occasions to wear tailored clothing, so they buy less; and usually they will buy a suit before an odd jacket because they judge suits to be more appropriate for those few occasions when a tie is required; and if they buy a jacket, it will be a blue blazer, be-cause it is familiar and so easily worn with "business casual."

I do not mean to blame the blazer, which is a necessity in every man's wardrobe. But you must know that there are two kinds of odd jackets: blazers, and all the others. The first are proper for occasions where dandification is unwelcome; the second can be worn everywhere else. And because one should never squander an opportunity for dandification, one must have recourse to the second. Therefore it is necessary for a man to know how to take advantage of the infinite range of colors, fabrics, and patterns that odd jackets offer. Classic film stars such as Astaire, Cooper, Ladd, and Tyrone Power always wore odd jackets in every scene where a suit was not required by the depiction of business. For they knew that odd jackets are worn when suits are not necessary but a tie is expected. Thus since a man, if he wants to dress well, is compelled of necessity to own various jacketings, he should pick tweeds and linens, because tweeds will keep you warm in winter and linen and its blends will keep you cool in summer. So one needs some tweeds and linens to outdress the multitude, and a blazer to placate the fuddy-duddies. Those who stay simply with the blazer do not understand this.

Among those who understood were the great jazz musicians—Armstrong, Ellington, and Basie, and also Sinatra before he took to wearing a dinner jacket even in the daytime. They never or rarely had occasion to be formal, but they loved dandification. Thus you will often see them in odd jackets, and rarely in blazers but rather in the boldest checks and most whimsical combinations. For they knew that colors too bold or numerous and patterns too large-scaled for suits are nonetheless welcome for odd jackets. And being in show business, they had much greater leeway for dandification than the rest of us. In our time, Wynton Marsalis keeps this tradition alive. And it is said that he is so fastidious that he always irons his own clothes before he performs; and this not only ensures that he looks good, but helps him scrape the mold off his brain and focus on his music.

As to how you should wear them, the most important thing is to create contrast; wearing jacket and trousers that look too much alike makes you look as though you put your clothes on in a daze, thinking they were part of the same suit. Contrast can be achieved through varying fabric, pattern, and color. Smooth tropical worsteds contrast nicely with the dryness of linen, while the ribbed texture of corduroy goes well with tweed. Patterned jackets go well with solid trousers, and vice versa. For, because patterns on odd jackets and trousers are bold, as was said, combining them hurts people's eyes and makes them angry at you. And even if one or the other pattern is small in scale, you should not try to mix them, because the risk is too great. Besides, the effect desired can just as easily be achieved by wearing boldly checked trousers with a solid jacket; for since these are so rare, they make you stand out as much as a two-pattern combination, but with less risk of ruin. As for color, gray trousers go with all but gray jackets, which take brown, blue, or white trousers. Shades of the same color may be worn together if they are vastly different: for instance, brown cavalry twill trousers will work with a brown and tan houndstooth jacket so long as the shade of the trousers is either much lighter or much darker than the ground of the jacket.

But let us come to the garments that you will need and what modes they should be. First, you should think of them in two modes, summer and winter, because no odd jacket is versatile enough to wear in more than three seasons, and the best of them are appropriate only in two. But if you have a few of the one and a few of the other, you will be prepared for any season and any weather, and you will always look better than those who believe what salesmen say about "year-round fabrics."

Tweeds are best for winter, and range in hand from the softest Shetlands to the hardest cheviots, and in heft from the thickest Harris tweeds to the thinnest thornproofs; but even the latter, because they are so tightly woven, will be too hot to wear before the fall. Except for Donegals, which are made in Western Ireland, all the best tweeds are hand-woven on ancient shuttle looms in Scotland. Shetland—which is named for the islands that are home to the sheep from which it is shorn, not after the ponies who also graze there—is considered by many to be the perfect tweed because it manages to be warm without being too thick and soft and spongy without requiring an infusion of cashmere, which, though it makes for beautiful odd jackets, costs more than your car and wears out much faster. But Shetland is too soft and delicate for trousers, whereas Donegals and cheviots are strong enough to withstand the stresses of sitting and walking.

Solid tweeds are never truly solid but "heathered," the effect achieved when threads of differing colors are mixed in small proportions to the ground. The most distinctive of all is "lovat," an indescribable blue-green made by mixing yarns of five different colors in proportions according to an ancient formula. And while tweeds are never woven with stripes (for these are appropriate only for suitings) they are made in the widest variety of patterns, from barleycorns to houndstooths to herringbones to shepherds checks to windowpanes to infinite varieties of plaid. Many of these originated as the proprietary pattern of an individual Scottish family, hence the term "estate tweeds" (which are also sometimes called "district checks"). The most famous of these is the glenurquhart plaid, commonly shortened to glen plaid. David Windsor, when he was prince of Wales, popularized this pattern and created his own version, large in scale, rust-colored, with a dark blue border check. Russell, the largest of all plaids, is so bold and busy it looks as though it were designed to make the wearer visible for miles, so that his hunting colleagues do not accidentally shoot him.

Linens make the best summer jackets. In light colors, with patch pockets, and unlined, these are airy and elegant. Apart from the blazer, it is the only odd jacket that looks well double-breasted; the others—and especially tweeds—must always be single. Silk and its blends sometimes make good spring jackets, but you must have two concerns. First, know that silk is hot, despite its reputation as perfect for summer. Second, few silk jacketings are woven with any taste and care must be taken in their selection lest you end up looking like Bugsy Siegel on his way to Las Vegas.

As to detailing, the buttons on odd jackets traditionally have only two holes drilled in them, whereas those on suits have four; the idea being that two-hole buttons are sportier. Sportier jackets might have turned-back sleeve cuffs that evoke tailored clothing's equine ancestry. The boldest dandies even have these put on their suit jackets. Other countrified details like throatlatches and crescent or slanted pockets (also called "hacking pockets," because their original purpose was to make accessing pockets easier while on horseback) should never be seen on suits, except perhaps tweeds, but can add distinction to odd jackets. I caution against leather patches on the elbows, unless indeed your jacket is so old that the sleeves really are worn through and it is so dear that you cannot bear to part with it. But details must be subtle and few. The bellows pockets (for shotgun shells), reinforced shoulders (to cushion the gun's recoil), and bi-swing backs (which facilitate quicker aiming) of Norfolk jackets are charming; but unless you have an estate in the Highlands where you shoot grouse, wearing one might subject you to unnecessary ridicule.

For trousers, I can make no stronger recommendation than medium-gray flannel. For nothing is more versatile or more stylish; you will have infinite opportunities to wear them, and when you do, you will always look good. And among those who understood this, the greatest was Fred Astaire, who was so often seen in gray flannels that when he gave a signed photo of himself to Audrey Hepburn (to commemorate a film they had made together), she had its frame covered in gray flannel so as to better remember him. But anything heavy will do, and if you have one pair of gray flannels, one pair of brown cavalry twills, and one pair of olive corduroys, you will be properly outfitted for any winter jacket. If you cannot be satisfied with these alone, you could try moleskin (a dense, heavy cotton) or whipcord (a tight woolen twill). For summer, linen and cotton twill in light colors will complement most any lightweight jacket. Pale flannels were popular in classic times, but most men today will find them too hot for warm weather.

In fall and winter, you might also consider adding an odd vest to your ensembles, for these add style in addition to helping you keep warm. There are two kinds: knitted (or sweater) and tailored. Knitted vests, which may be pull-over or button-up, are informal but somewhat dandified. In solids, they are useful and versatile; when patterned, limited but rakish. Both look best when, rather than being smooth, some texture is woven into the cloth. And though Italian dandies like Agnelli would wear crewnecks with ties, most men are better served by a deep V neck that mimics the opening of a tailored vest. These latter are typically made from wool in some classic pattern, such as tattersall, but may also be solid. The most renowned color is hunting pink (which is really scarlet), but this is appropriate only for fox hunting. Yellow and green are also seen, but these could make you look like a hobbit, and in any case will look out of place anywhere but in the countryside. Far more versatile is one in brown suede; for this goes with most anything and always adds a rich luster. Fancier vests are available, but can only be worn with solid jackets, and since patterned tweeds are much more interesting than solids, you will have fewer opportunities to wear them.

Unless you own a blazer; and dandies will want two: one in flannel or serge for the winter, and one in hopsack or fresco for spring and summer. For dandies have always loved the blazer because it is the one odd jacket that ought to be double-breasted, reflecting the garment's origins as a naval uniform. Whether its name originated from Queen Victoria's inspection of the frigate H.M.S. *Blazer* in 1837—when it is said that the captain, dismayed at the slovenliness of his crew, had them all outfitted in crisp blue jackets before Her Majesty's arrival—or whether it started with the jackets worn by a Cambridge rowing crew that were so brightly colored they were said to "blaze," no one can prove. And although you will many times hear people refer to any and all odd jackets as blazers, this is an error. For the term refers only to solid navy ones; the American forest green version is acceptable only if you have won the Masters, and burgundy only in the Bahamas.

True blazers must have metal buttons; a blue jacket with horn buttons can be most elegant, but it is not a blazer. Indeed, blazers are the only jackets of any kind to take metal buttons; and though they are most often in brass, they may also be of silver or gold. If your school makes blazer buttons with its seal, or you belong to some club or branch of the military that does the same, it is fitting to have your tailor sew these buttons on your jacket. If not, your buttons must be plain, or else of some subtle pattern. And as it is commonplace to see men wearing blazers whose buttons bear the bogus crest of some designer, with its simple buttons your blazer will be recognized as the more elegant.

And here it is to be noted that the classic blazer is double-breasted, with four instead of six buttons (arranged like a square, so that two can actually button), side vents, and patch pockets, to reflect its naval origins (for whichever story is true, its ancestor the reefer jacket was born on the water, and it has been the jacket of boaters for more than a century). Its shade should be a touch lighter than suiting navy, and its weave a little more textured. While ticket pockets are acceptable and even desirable on all other odd jackets, they are incorrect on blazers. The single-breasted blazer is acceptable, but only in flannel, with three buttons, three open patch pockets, and side vents. By all means you should avoid the ubiquitous worsted, two-button, center-vented version; for since odd jackets afford you the chance to wear many stylish details that cannot be worn on suits, it is not reasonable to forgo these in favor of one that looks all but identical to a run-of-the-mill suit jacket. Know well also that the English consider the blazer to be yachting regalia, or perhaps something to be worn once a year to the Henley Regatta. When they see it in town, they assume the wearer is American.

Blazers are most useful because they can be worn with any odd trousers except navy blue, as was said. The classic complement to a blazer is "white ducks," which are neither white nor in any way related to ducks. For instead of "dead white," they are off white, looking "as though they've been stored away in the bottom of a trunk for fifteen or twenty years." Traditionally made of canvas ("duck" is a corruption of "doek," the original Dutch word for "canvas"), they are in our time more commonly found in linen or gabardine or flannel, and the cloth you will want will depend on the season and your tolerance for warmth. I recommend against wearing khakis with your blazer because, although they complement each other well enough, they are worn by everyone, especially the young, who own nothing else. To wear them together either betrays a lack of imagination, or else will make people think you are from California. For, because that state is so informal, the men there think that all a shirt needs to make it formal is a collar, and a jacket with lapels is well nigh black tie. Whence is derived the phrase "California Tux," for when they hear the word "formal," they automatically reach for their blazer and khakis, the pinnacle of their wardrobe. And we should expect nothing more from the state that gave us "business casual."

Nonetheless, khakis are useful for your other summer jackets, because the dullness of cotton equally complements the sheen of silk, the crispness of tropical worsted, and the dryness of linen. And a variety of summer jackets in these cloths, or some blend thereof, will serve you well. Most of the patterns found in tweeds are also found in these odd jackets but in lighter and brighter colors. Some particularly vivid solid shades, woven in linen or silk, make exceptionally dandified summer jackets, but these are wearable only in tropical climes, which for most men means only on vacation.

And although I have discussed them at length above, I must add a word here about shoes. Black shoes are not worn with odd jackets but only with suits. The sole exception might be black monk straps with a blazer, gray trousers, and a formal shirt and tie—a look favored by the Parisians, who think that it combines the formality of a suit with the dandification of an odd jacket. But you can never go wrong with brown suede. Otherwise, brown calf or burgundy cordovan are to be preferred in winter, and brown or tan calf or white suede in summer. The white buck—a suede oxford with red rubber soles—is a most dandified and smart shoe; with a blazer and white ducks, it is the height of style. Aside from these, lace-ups are rarely worn, and only the less formal models, such as bluchers and split-toes with flannels and tweeds. Conversely, monk-straps and slip-ons go well with lighter cloths.

It does not appear to me that I can leave out a discussion of "business casual." For, though contemptible, it nonetheless is common in our time, and one must live in one's time. Some trace its beginnings to the century-old English practice of excusing brown tweed suits in town on Fridays, at the end of which so many gentlemen headed to the country. But that practice died long before the invention by American corporations of "casual Friday," which was the forerunner of "business casual," which caused the first recession of the 21st century. And to better illustrate its dangers, I note that after the accounting firm Arthur

Anderson introduced it into England, Savile Row tailor Angus Cundy predicted that it would cause their ruin—and soon after, the firm imploded in the Enron scandal. Thus, if you work in an environment where "business casual" is decreed, I recommend that you wear suits to do your part to kill off this unfortunate trend and save the global economy. But if you have no choice, because holding the line would impede your career, you should always heed the wise counsel of Flusser that all men's attire is built around some sort of coat. And I do not recommend leather jackets with turtlenecks or the like. Men who think that by wearing them they will look like Steve McQueen in *Bullitt* deceive themselves, for in not being McQueen you will not look like him but like a weekend hipster trying to impress his new cookie. Yet odd jackets are useful, and especially blazers, because they can be worn without ties, while nonetheless elevating the dignity of your appearance above a polo shirt and rumpled chinos—unless you dress with the dishevelment of Woody Allen, whose tweeds look like upholstery ripped from a decrepit sofa. But if worn with crisply pressed trousers, a respectable shirt, and shoes that can hold a shine, odd jackets will make you look not only more businesslike and less casual, but almost good.

XXI.

Of Neckwear

The first conjecture that is made of the style of a man is to see his ties, for these "come into the room almost before the man"; and when they are tasteful and suitable, he will always be reputed smart because he has known how to recognize them as tasteful and to wear them when suitable. But if they are otherwise, one can always pass unfavorable judgment on his tastes, because the first error he makes, he makes in this choice.

There is no one who sees the neckties of Bill Clinton who does not judge him to be a most well-dressed man, because he wears such exemplary ties and always selects the right one for the right purpose. And since there are six kinds of ties, each with its own character and level of formality: club, striped, spotted, geometric, solid, and all other kinds; the first two are less formal, the next three more so, and the last vulgar—it follows that Clinton knows how to buy good ties and how to wear the right one for specific occasions and with specific jackets and shirts. It is a measure of his great virtue in selecting neckties that he generally looks so presentable despite his shoddy, fashion-imbued suits.

And I say that the necktie is the linchpin of the modern wardrobe. Almost every article of clothing we wear is designed to be worn either with it or without it, and its presence or absence is the first rule of every written and unwritten dress code. When the tie finally dies, tailored clothing will not long outlive it. And the reason is that it is the one article of pure ceremony that survived Brummell's great purge of powdered wigs, buckled pumps, silk knee breeches, and brocaded coats—anything not offering warmth, protection, or comfort. Its sole function is to signify that we have risen so far above necessity that we can afford to buy beautiful pieces of silk and tie them around our necks without fear that they will be scorched in battle, torn in the hunt, or soiled by toil. But once it is gone, men's willingness to tolerate ceremony in their clothes will erode still further, and they will look at their dress shirts and say "surely there are easier and more comfortable ways to cover a torso than this," and at their suits and think "couldn't a windbreaker keep me just as warm at a fraction of the cost?"

The origin of the tie is unknown, though theories abound, some tracing it as far back as ancient Rome. The most popular holds it to be descended from the neckcloths worn by Croatian soldiers in the 17th century, and that the word *cravat*—what the French call a necktie—is a corruption of "croat." Certainly, the tie we wear today is an offspring of the starched white neckcloth popularized by Brummell in the early 19th century. And from his time to ours, being fully dressed has required a tie.

But as to how a man can know what is a good necktie and which kind is appropriate with which combination of jacket and shirt, here are some rules that never fail. The best ties are made entirely of silk, for silk is more durable, lustrous, and resilient than other fabrics. Nonetheless, wool and cashmere ties pair nicely with flannels and tweeds in the winter, while linen, linen-silk blends, and Irish poplin (a mix of silk and wool) make wonderful ties for summer. No other fabrics will do. For the lining, only wool makes a good knot and returns to its original shape after untying, readying itself for the tie's next foray around your neck. Good ties are also made by hand; for a handmade tie is never stiff and lifeless, like machine-made ties, but always fluid and springy. And if not the whole tie is stitched by hand, then at least the fold on the underside must be closed at each end with hand-sewn bar tacks, and the spine must be sewn by hand with a "slip stitch," a loose thread that holds the tie together while allowing its shape to give with wear yet always return to normal when untied. On better ties, the loop that keeps the narrow end (or "blade") in place will be of the same material as the body (or "shell") of the tie, and this loop will be tucked into the rear seam of the front blade. And a self-loop is the only proper keeper; manufacturer's labels, which are far more common, snag threads from woven ties, causing them to fray. The covering for the underside of each end, or "tipping," will be of self-material as well. Yet the very finest ties are not tipped at all but made from a single square yard of silk folded seven times with no wool lining, so that only the silk itself gives the tie its heft. Most ties used to be made in this mode, but the cost of silk and the lack of skilled artisans make them rare and expensive in our time. Slightly more common are the so-called double-four-folds, the guts of which look something like seven-folds except that they use less silk and are both lined and tipped. The benefits of these refinements are more psychological than sartorial, as only the wearer will ever see them, and only if he turns over his tie and pulls it open. As to width, fashion dictates that this change frequently, as if standards of aesthetics varied from year to year. Sometimes ties are made as wide as lobster bibs, other times as narrow as shirt plackets. The traditional width of an English regimental tie is three and a quarter inches, and that is as narrow as a tie should be. At the other end of the scale, the Italians have always favored wider ties, and the exuberance common to that people has often led them to excess in this matter. And though their ties are otherwise the world's finest, you must be cautious when selecting one that its width not exceed four inches, the utmost limit of propriety.

When choosing which tie to wear with what shirt and jacket, there are two chief considerations: color and formality. As to the former, the predominant color of the tie must reflect some color in your shirt or jacket, or else be complementary to both, for example a yellow tie with a blue blazer and a blue-and-white shirt. If the tie is a mix of two or more equally prominent colors, then at least one of them must reflect a color in the shirt or jacket, and the others cannot be offensive to either; or else if different, all of the tie's colors must complement both shirt and jacket. Ties with three or more colors achieve their greatest effect when placed in discreet surroundings; the combination of a many-colored tie with a many-colored shirt or jacket tends toward the garish. Nonetheless those with great experience in sartorial matters have shown that it can be done well if sufficient respect is paid to which colors complement and which offend one another. An education in this can be had by watching Ed Hayes on Court TV. He loves mixing colors and patterns so much that he rarely wears solids, and always looks lively and stylish. Well-dressed men also vary the color of their ties with the changing of the seasons, wearing bright, vibrant colors more in spring and summer, and more muted, darker tones in fall and winter.

Formality intersects with color in that darker ties are generally more formal than lighter ones. But the true measure of a tie's formality is its kind; and a light-colored tie of a formal kind is more formal than a dark-colored one of a less formal kind. And no matter what its kind, silk ties are always more formal than ties made from linen or wool or cashmere. Knitted sock ties with straight bottom edges are the least formal of all, go well with button down collars, and are appropriate only with odd jackets or perhaps informal tweed suits. Club ties—those with small insignia embroidered onto a solid ground—are next. If the insignia on the tie represents a specific club or school to which you have no connection, you should not wear it. But many club ties have pictures of animals or sports equipment or other whimsical things. The Adam Smith tie, ubiquitous among conservative ideologues, is but the best-known example.

Striped ties are intrinsically informal, but depending on their color and what they are worn with, they can effect a more formal look. Eminently versatile, and an elegant accompaniment to a checked shirt, striped ties are necessary for every man, but especially helpful for narrowing wide faces and sharpening soft ones.

Born in England as the sartorial symbol of a particular regiment or school, there are as many striped ties as there are regiments and schools, and many more besides that have no connection to any organization but were dreamed up by some designer. The English look with contempt, and sometimes anger, on the sight of a non-belonger wearing the former kind; thus you should never wear them in England. But Americans not only do not care, they do not even notice, so that wearing them here will not harm you. Better, however, is to wear Italian examples, which not only never correspond to a regiment or school, but also infuse some surface interest into the silk—for instance by varying the weave of the stripe from that of the ground—whereas English stripes are always made from plain repp (or corded) silk. Traditionally, the stripes descend from left to right. Some say this is to match the left-over-right fastening of men's jackets, a practice which originated in the age of swordplay: because most men are right-handed, they wore their swords on the left, necessitating that the buttons be on the right; whereas the buttons on women's coats have always been on the left. When Brooks Brothers introduced the repp tie to America, they deliberately made their stripes go the other way to distinguish them from English regimentals. But I believe that the original mode looks better, because a jacket's breast pocket is always on the left side, and every well-dressed man always has a handkerchief therein; and stripes that descend from left to right form a clean line for the eye to follow, whereas stripes that go the other way create a trough.

With spotted ties we reach the threshold of formality. For there are few spotted ties that can be worn with a button down shirt, and that is as good a measure of a tie's formality as any. I say then that only ties on which the spots are printed and not woven (for embroidery makes any tie more formal), and are at least an inch apart, can be so worn. All others demand more formal shirts. Yet they are nonetheless most versatile, and you ought to have a good many of them in your closet, some bright, some dark; some printed, some embroidered; and some with closely spaced, minute dots, some with fewer, larger dots. But know well that if you plan to wear a tie with spots as big as even the smallest coin, as Molloy noted in his only useful bit of advice, these demand the proper accessories: red nose, floppy shoes, propeller beanie, and squirting boutonnière. Geometrics—such as checks, plaids, lattice weaves, diamonds, grids, and other small patterns—are more formal still, especially if they are woven. Such silks used to be the specialty of French Huguenot weavers who settled in the English parish of Macclesfield after being expelled by Louis XIV when he revoked the Edict of Nantes. And ties with small, neat, all-over patterns made by tightly weaving different colored threads are in our time still called Macclesfields. In black and white or silver, the English call them wedding ties and wear them to festive formal occasions. A similar weave, but larger in scale and thus slightly less formal, are named for the East London parish of Spitalsfield, where they were woven for many years. One sees both on President Clinton, but also on any man concerned with style. They should be worn only with suits, rarely with light suits, and never with button down collars. Nor should solids (except sock ties), which are so rarely seen in our time that their effect is always striking. The most excellent wearer of them was Cary Grant, who wore nothing else, and somehow managed—despite always wearing them with white shirts and plain suits—never to look boring. In such surroundings, they are the most formal of all ties; but they also make wonderful companions for intricately striped and checked shirts, which can be paired with multi-colored, wildly patterned ties only with great difficulty and at great risk. In our time, Geoff Colvin wears them to good effect, as did saloon singer Bobby Short when he was not in black tie, knowing that when both jacket and shirt are vividly patterned, solid ties are a necessity. Smooth silks, like the satins favored by Grant, make for a more formal look; but textured weaves like grenadines and twills add character to the tie.

Of the remaining ties, the greatest number by far display irregular and unsightly patterns printed on silk that "leap out in front of shirts, as if to announce the awkwardness of the wearer." They are popular because men believe that in order to look distinct they must wear a garish tie, and the kinds discussed above they consider too staid to be sharp. And this error is so common that one often sees men whose habits of dress are held in high esteem solely because they always wear a particular brand of expensive, printed French tie. But such men cannot be considered well dressed, because in adhering so slavishly to one kind of tie they deprive themselves of five-sixths of the necktie universe, and also because they do not understand that it is the quality and cut of one's clothes coupled with the judicious blending of colors, fabrics, and patterns that make one look sharp and not ties that resemble Jackson Pollock paintings or Times Square advertisements. And if someone should say: but not all printed ties are vulgar, I respond: either the ties are multi-colored and wildly patterned or they have subtly colored, discreet, all-over patterns printed on heavy, beautifully draping English silk twill. In the first case they are vulgar; in the second they may not be. But so few are not, and the ability to recognize these is given to so few, that it is safer to avoid them altogether.

Lest I be accused of leaving out three important considerations, I want to mention them here: and they are bow ties, knots, and care. As to the first, it is true that the multitude considers bow tie wearers odd or at best professorial, so that if you are not a professor and do not wish to be taken for one, and are not so eminent that it does not matter what you wear, you must be careful to wear them only in whimsical situations, and preferably with odd jackets and trousers (more preferably still with flannels and tweeds). As examples, I wish to cite one from classic times and three from our own. The late Senator Paul Simon of Illinois always wore bow ties and was universally regarded as a nerd. Arthur M. Schlesinger, Jr., also favors bow ties, but because he really is a professor, he does not suffer for it. George Will used to wear them exclusively but got tired of being known more for his ties than his writing and so gave them up. Winston Churchill always wore a navy-blue, woven-spotted bow tie, but he had so much reputation that on him they were considered endearing. Also, like all successful bow tie wearers, he knew that because they do not cover the shirt buttons and thus leave a great void in one's middle, they are best worn with a vest, and always in the case of suits. And neither he nor any other man who wishes to avoid ignominy would ever wear one pre-tied, but always learns to tie them himself, for a pre-tied bow tie is too perfect and thus fake-looking, while the slightly disheveled look of a hand-tied bow tie imparts character.

I shall not discuss the mechanics of tying a tie because that subject has been amply treated elsewhere, and besides, if you do not know how to tie a tie, you need to start with a different book. But I will say that large knots are only appropriate with spread- or cutaway-collars, and only for those men with thick necks and large heads. And even then they are not always necessary, and sometimes counterproductive, because certain ties, especially wovens and grenadines, make large knots even when you use a four-in-hand (by far the most common knot) while Windsor knots will look too big, too wide, and too symmetrical. And you should know that the duke himself did not wear them, but had his ties bespoke with thick silk and thicker linings. The eponymous knot was invented by someone who sought to copy the duke's look but did not understand that it derived not from the knot but from the construction of his ties. Most men contrive their knots so that there is a small dimple in the center of the tie just below the knot, which helps the front blade drape properly. Others believe that dimples smack of too much artifice and follow the duke in favoring a soft, dimpleless rounded knot, which is actually harder to tie. As to care, you should always untie your tie by reversing the knot rather than pulling the small end through, as this stretches and warps the silk. Also, if a spot appears on your tie, rub it out with the narrow end of the tie. As ties do not respond well to dry-cleaning, if this does not work, the tie is likely ruined. You should always have enough ties so that the ruin of one does not force you to wear the same few over and over. Yet you need not go so far as Brian Williams, of whom it is said that he never wears the same tie on the air twice. Nor should you save every riotous or insipid graduation or Father's Day gift tie. The duke of Windsor used to weed through his ties at the end of every year, removing any that he had not worn in the prior year and keeping his collection to an even 50. But the English have always preferred shirts to ties, and 50 is probably too few for an American dandy.

When, therefore, shirt, jacket, and tie are so constituted that all work together in harmony with respect to color and formality, their wearer will benefit. If they are otherwise, the end is always damaging to him.

XXII.

Whether Suspenders and Many Other Things Which Are Bought and Worn by Dandies Every Day Are Tasteful or Tasteless

Some dandies wear suspenders to hold up their trousers securely; some others resort to belts; some wear handkerchiefs in their breast pockets; some others omit them; some wear topcoats in winter and hats all year round; and still others wear collar pins, tie clips, and other ornaments. And although one cannot give a definite judgment on all these things unless one comes to the particulars of the person wearing them and what they are worn with, nonetheless I shall speak in that broad mode which the matter permits.

There has never been, then, a well-dressed man who has not worn suspenders; on the contrary, he has always worn them. For since the trousers of dandies are cut with a long rise, to be worn at the natural waist, they require them. And without them, such trousers will not remain where they belong or hang properly. But when they are worn, you never have to worry about your trousers slipping, even if you wear them an inch or so too large in the waist, which is more comfortable; and you will never be seen hiking them up. But if your trousers are cut so that they rest on your hips—as are most ready-made American and nearly all Italian trousers—then suspenders are harmful: for such trousers sit below the protrusion of your belly (and rare is the man whose belly protrudes not at all) and the suspenders must arc around it, making you look even fatter than you actually are. I wish I did not need to specify that suspenders are always buttoned to your trousers, never clipped. Yet according to a common opinion, "suspenders" properly refers to trouser supports that clip onto the waistband while "braces" refers to those that button via small strips of leather. But this is an error, and the two terms mean the same thing; the former is used by Americans while the latter is preferred by the English. The color of the ends should always reflect the color of your shoes. Nonetheless, the white gut ends made by Albert Thurston, the world's finest manufacturer of suspenders, go marvelously with black shoes and even with brown suede. Suspenders offer infinite ways to refine your ensembles through an additional dash of color or fabric or pattern or some combination thereof. Most are made either of silk or rayon or boxcloth. Silk is not recommended, because it does not last; rayon, while unnatural, is nonetheless hardwearing and long-lived; fuzzy boxcloth is ideal for winter suitings. Some rules that men find useful: suspenders' color should reflect another piece of your ensemble, generally the tie or the suit, or else contrast yet coordinate, such as burgundy paired with blue; solid suspenders are to be preferred with busy shirts, while patterns go better with solid shirts; striped suspenders look best with patterned or solid ties, whereas other patterns better complement striped ties. Those who are esteemed wise used to say that because suspenders were considered akin to underwear, it was gauche to display them in public. But their great vogue among Wall Streeters in the 1980s and their ubiquity on talk show host Larry King have done much to dispel this sentiment. But the English still cling to it; and many others find suspenders pretentious, especially on the young, as was said, so you may need to use caution when wearing them.

Belts are everywhere inoffensive but always uncomfortable. For instead of just the soft cloth of a waistband, your belly confronts an inflexible strip of leather that must be cinched tight if it is to perform its function. While you are standing it is uncomfortable, and when you are sitting intolerable. And it does not perform its function but requires of you constant adjustments when it allows your pants to slip down too low, which is always. Nonetheless, if trousers are cut higher than the hips yet slightly lower than the waist, and if the front and back rise are just right and the sides properly tapered inward, they will stay up without cinching, making a belt purely decorative. And since some men find suspenders' extra straps of cloth intolerable in summer, these can be a godsend. Whether it is worn to cinch or for show, a belt's leather and color should reflect those of your shoes, and its buckle should be smallish and discreet.

Without doubt your ensembles become great with the addition of a pocket handkerchief. Lacking one, you cannot be considered fully dressed, much less well dressed. But most men, thinking them affected, are afraid of them. Nonetheless, three men who for decades depended on their reputations for their livelihoods and prestige—Tom Brokaw, Peter Jennings, and Dan Rather—always wore them, to no ill effect. If they could, then certainly you can. But it is true that in the most hidebound and hierarchical industries and environments, wearing them is customarily reserved for those who have attained eminence by virtue of their title, their accomplishments, or their character. And I wish one example to suffice. Michael Lewis writes of the investment banking industry that only partners ever wore handkerchiefs and only managing directors suspenders, and that those who wore them without attaining the necessary rank were considered insolent, and if they persisted in wearing them after being rebuked, they were ruined. An ambitious man, then, cannot wear them, nor should he, if his environment is against them. And if the maxim "Dress for the job you want" were good, this teaching would not be good; but because men are envious and often consider attempts to dress like themselves to be presumptuous, it will always be necessary for you to assess the customs of your workplace and dress accordingly. But, to continue, I say that there are three kinds of handkerchiefs: solid or woven linen or cotton, printed silk or wool, and those that match your tie. The first are most excellent, the second excellent, the third useless. White linen goes with everything, and elevates even the most woeful jacket. Dyed Swiss cotton, in various subtle colors, goes well with shirts of similar hues, and so should always be near at hand. Without endorsing the rule which says that shiny ties must be worn with dull pocket squares and vice versa, I agree that the smoothness of silk makes a nice counterpoise to richly woven ties as well as those of dry wool and linen;

while wool pocket squares complement winter clothing. And the livelier patterns available in these can brighten an otherwise stale ensemble. Brit Hume always wears a patterned silk handkerchief and always looks rakish. But you must eschew handkerchiefs that match your tie. For these are nothing but Garanimals for adults; to wear them is to shout to the world that you do not know how to dress yourself; and the only parts of any ensemble that should ever match are your two shoes and your two socks. As to how handkerchiefs should be employed, there are two rules: first, they should be angled up toward your left shoulder, because this accentuates the flattering V illusion created for your torso by your tailored jacket; and second, they should look as though they were thrust into your pocket haphazardly, to give your clothes a nonchalant air, although, as with everything else regarding your dress, there can be nothing haphazard about it. This principle was taught by Brummell when he wrote:

> *My neckcloth, of course, forms my principal care,*
> *For by that we criterions of elegance swear,*
> *And it costs me each morning some hours of flurry,*
> *To make it appear to be tied in a hurry.*

The ties of our era do not take well to being tied in this manner, so dandies have devolved this noble pretense onto their handkerchiefs. Learning to fold and place a handkerchief is best accomplished through trial and error; but it helps to know how to form the four basic folds: the four-point, the triangle, the square, and the puff. And, while recognizing that certain textures and certain folds seem to complement each other best (such as linen and the four-point, or silk and the puff), dandies have always experimented with their own folds. Many have learned to create rakish and unique examples that redound to their glory and even enter the pantheon of style, as it is said that Fred Astaire invented the puff. You should never buy handkerchiefs that are pre-folded; for, aside from the surrender that this signifies, in being too precise they will never achieve that haphazard nonchalance that is the hallmark of style.

Overcoats are necessary in the bitter cold and can impart some style if chosen judiciously. The plain single-breasted, notched lapel coat, in a dark color, is the most common; double-breasted (always with peaked lapels), it is a bit more dandified. The Chesterfield may also be single- or double-breasted. It is more tailored and shaped than most, and thus made of lighter cloth, typically blue or gray herringbone. Because of its weight, it is sometimes generally called a topcoat, but this term properly refers to any lightweight overcoat. A true Chesterfield always has a velvet collar and a breast welt pocket meant for a handkerchief; and if single-breasted, it takes a fly-front. The covert coat is single-breasted with a fly-front, but unlike the Chesterfield, it is made from a sturdy twill—called "covert cloth"—of tightly woven brown, tan, and cream threads that combine to form a mottled light brown called "fawn." The polo coat is double-breasted with envelope pockets, cuffed sleeves, and a half belt (sometimes called a "martingale") in back. Traditionally, it was made of camel hair; but other cloths and blends are acceptable so long as the color is tan. Also double-breasted, the Ulster has wide, rounded lapels that cannot be called peaked because they point downward, but cannot be called notched because collar and lapels sit flush, with the bottom edge of the collar being just as long as the top of the lapels. Always single-breasted, the Raglan has no shoulder seams but sleeve seams that run all the way to the collar, giving the shoulder a rounded, casual shape. And the collar itself is a "ghillie"—pointy like a shirt collar, not squarish like a typical coat collar. There are other models, but these have endured and will endure, and can see a man through any situation. A plain coat in black or dark gray or blue can be worn with almost anything, and is the first choice of a prudent man when buying his first overcoat. The Chesterfield also goes well with business suits and formal clothes, but is too formal to be worn with tweed suits or odd jackets. The polo and Ulster are spiffy enough to be worn with a suit and sporty enough for a tweed jacket. Daring men and insouciant WASPs will wear the polo with a dinner jacket, but the hidebound consider this a sacrilege. The Raglan is the least formal overcoat that can be worn with a tie, and is the perfect covering for tweed jackets. Sturdy, inexpensive coats are made of wool; but cashmere is finer, and because it is more insulating, it can be worn in lighter weights. Alpaca and vicuña are finer still, but more delicate and prohibitively expensive. Tweeds make a nice, countrified coat and offer excellent protection from the rain. But they do not complement worsted suits, which in inclement weather require a simple tan raincoat of tightly woven cotton. Trench coats are for trenches. A topcoat should fit much like a jacket, only more loosely, to accommodate the layers beneath. It should be long enough to cover the knee and finish about mid-calf; any shorter, it looks like a child's coat; any longer, like a ball gown. Its sleeves should be long enough to cover jacket sleeves and shirt cuffs alike. With the exception of the magnificent but archaic paddock coat (once the preferred outwear for formal clothes), all topcoats, even double-breasted ones, are center-vented, and the vent should culminate below your seat.

Hats are a problem for the dandy. They are marvelously dandified and can add an exclamation point to an already superb ensemble, and also a dash of color: many dandies will liven up a staid gray suit with brown suede shoes and a brown felt hat. But they can be uncomfortable to wear, because they bind your scalp, mash down your hair, and trap heat that your head is trying to expel. And this was the opinion of Kennedy, who wore them only when forced to; and since his time they have been considered so old-fashioned and out-of-date as to be almost costume. Yet to see that they look good, you have only to see them on Willie Brown, who wears hats every day with great aplomb. But he is bald, so he need not worry about his hair; and he lives in San Francisco, so is not bothered by heat and has nothing to fear from dandification. But if you want to wear them, you should know that they range in formality from tweed caps for winter and straw boaters for summer, to the top hat, which will be discussed in its place. The best town hats are made from beaver felt, and the dressiest business model is the homburg, which is stiff with a upturned brim. It is proper in black or gray (though Tom Wolfe has his made in white, to match his suits) and should only be worn with the most formal ensembles, such as what Churchill and Eden wore with theirs. Leaving aside the bowler or derby (the hat worn by Steed), which in our time is costume, the next formal is the fedora, often seen on Bogart and other film stars in classic times. It is appropriate with most suits, provided its color is complementary. Brown, blue, and gray are best, but I have even seen green examples which I could not help but admire. The porkpie, a favorite of Astaire and Sinatra, has a narrower brim but a higher crown, and is slightly less formal than the fedora and also more rare. Similar to the fedora, but softer, and with a narrower brim and band, is the trilby—though because of its equestrian heritage this is more appropriate with tweeds and odd jackets. For this reason, I recommend that these be brown, though pearl gray examples are also seen. The Panama, genuine examples of which are made in Ecuador, is hand woven from palm leaves in many shapes, some—like the Montecristi—unique to this material. It is much cooler than any felt hat, and thus is welcome in summer, but it is still covering your head, so it will nonetheless make you hot. And so will the boater, a much stiffer hat made of straw. These above are proper with town suits. Tweed caps can be worn with tweed suits or with heavier odd jackets and trousers. Linen caps go well with summer suitings and jacketings. When choosing a hat, you should also think about the shape of your face. Just as rounded shirt collars emphasize a rounded face, making it look egg-like, so too do low-crown, rounded hats. These make a nice contrast with long, slender faces; roundheads should stick with squared-off hats with high crowns.

It has been the custom of gentlemen, so as not to look vulgar, to eschew jewelry. Nonetheless, many prefer to clip their tie to their shirt with a device of gold or silver. This is acceptable, provided it is not garish or bejeweled (for gentlemen never wear jewels), and even recommended, because it helps you maintain a rakish arch to your tie and keeps it out of your soup. You should never let the clasp sit horizontally, however, as this bisects the body and deëmphasizes the vertical line—much better to angle it downward slightly. Collar pins are also acceptable, though a little fussy and more than a little dandified. They are of two varieties: those like safety pins, which puncture each side of a collar in order to close it; and those like dumbbells, which are inserted through eyelets and affixed with a screw and ball. True pins are more dashing, which is why they were favored by Fred Astaire, who amazingly wore them with button down collars; but they are hard to manipulate, and repeated punctures can cause a collar's surface to fray over time. Some men cheat by using a safety pin with eyelets; purists hold this practice in contempt, but I am willing to excuse small indiscretions undertaken for the sake of style. Those contrivances made to look like a real pin, but that simply clasp the edges of the collar, are in the same stylistic league as clip-on ties.

Watches and cufflinks are the only other jewelry-like indulgence permitted to the gentleman. The former should be slender and simple, with a leather band if worn on the wrist, or an antique chain if in a pocket. As to the latter, the English wear cufflinks ubiquitously and consider them required for business, whereas Italians reserve them for weddings and the like, preferring button cuffs for ordinary wear. The richer or more sartorially obsessed an American is, the more likely he is to wear them. They are available in an infinite variety, but plain silver is best, especially if you only have one pair, because, unlike patterned links, these can be worn with even the busiest patterned shirts as well as plain ones. But links with subtle patterns and colors can nicely complement some other part of your ensemble. You should always prefer true links—that is, two identical sides joined by a chain—to one side posted on a swivel. But if you are given presidential seal cufflinks by the president, by all means wear them, even though they are single-sided. And you can also wear a lapel pin representing a medal, provided it is a medal you have actually won. General Colin Powell always wears one, and no one ever criticizes him.

A boutonnière is the ultimate finishing touch for any dandy. The traditional flower is the carnation—white for weddings, funerals, and full dress occasions, red for everything else. Yellow or pink can be substituted to better match the colors of your ensemble, as might a blue cornflower if one can be found. Other flowers, while not out of the question, should be approached with caution. Expensive, elaborate florist creations that look like bouquets are for women. An iron rule is that if it has to be pinned to your lapel, it should not be worn. Gentlemen place the flower in their lapel buttonhole, and use a silk loop on the underside of the lapel to secure the stem.

So, having considered all these things, I shall praise whoever wears suspenders and whoever does not, and I shall blame anyone who, when not forced by necessity, omits a handkerchief, or who wears too much jewelry.

XXIII.

In What Modes Formal Wear
Is to Be Avoided

I do not want to leave out an important point and an error from which men defend themselves with difficulty, unless they are very prudent or well advised. And these are the corruptions to which formal clothes are subjected. For manufacturers, in their indolence and parsimony, do not respect tradition and make formal clothes that look just like business clothes. And because men do not know any better, they defend themselves with difficulty from this plague. In trying, they act nobly; but to succeed, they must understand that formal clothing is called "formal" not only because it is worn on formal occasions, but also because it preserves some form of clothing worn in the past. And for formal clothing to be correct, it must continue to preserve them; the gravity of the occasions to which they are worn demands nothing less. This is shown in the film *Swing Time,* when not one but two weddings are called off because the grooms committed the grave error of demanding cuffs on their formal trousers.

Wishing thus to discuss what are the origins of most formal clothes still worn in our time, I note that they arose from the English habit of dressing for dinner, a product of life in the country, where men spent a great part of the day on horseback. As Hardy Amies has written, "Personal hygiene apart, you did not want to bring the smell of the stables into the house." So men changed clothes before coming to the table; and this practice, because of its elegance, spread to the cities, then to the Continent, then to the *haut monde* (for, in sartorial matters, the whole world is an English colony). As to the garments themselves, some who have written of this say that all men's clothes derive either from military uniforms or sporting clothes. Some others, wiser it seems to me, have the opinion that all garments begin life as sports clothes worn in the country during the day, are adapted for the town, become acceptable for ceremonial wear in the evening, and finally are relegated to servants' uniforms. And because modes of dress vary two or three times every three or four hundred years, a garment is worn for light occasions in the country or grave ones in town but for a few decades.

These variations of garments arise out of a desire for comfort among men. For all the clothes we wear today began life on horseback, as was said. And because life in the saddle is strenuous, it demands freedom of movement. Thus did the squires of old abandon the doublet and hose worn at court in favor of more comfortable coats left long in back, but cut across the waist in front, so that excess cloth did not spill over the knees and saddle. It was Beau Brummell himself, prince of the dandies, who decades later first wore this coat in town; and because of his hold over the mind of the prince regent, it was not only accepted but became the fashion of the day, worn by everyone who could afford it and envied by those who could not. But even Brummell would not wear it at night, for this he considered too great a liberty, agreeing with his royal patron that the solemnity of evening demanded more courtly garments. But once Brummell was exiled to France, and George to the hereafter, men were emboldened to wear this tailcoat after dark. The squires saw an opening to wear something still more comfortable in the country and had their tailors devise a short jacket for riding, shooting, and everyday wear. And they began to wear it in the house, when smoking their after-dinner Havanas, so as not to befoul their evening clothes with the smell of tobacco, which offended their wives and mistresses. To further increase its comfort, they had this smoking jacket made in the same soft velvet as their dressing gowns. After this, it was a short step for them to ask that it be made in black wool, with tailcoat trimmings, so that it was dignified enough to be worn in the dining room. Thus was born the distinction between "formal" wear, or full evening dress, and "semi-formal" wear. The former meant the tailcoat, which in elevated circles was *de rigueur* at the dinner table every evening, and always at concerts, operas, theatres, balls, banquets, nightclubs, and smart restaurants. The latter allowed for the short dinner jacket and was acceptable in one's own home and at private clubs. Americans claim that tobacco heir Griswold Lorillard was the first to wear this jacket in the presence of ladies, at the 1886 Autumn Ball of the Tuxedo Park Club, where all the other men were in tails. The English claim that Grizzy's infamous jacket was a tailcoat with the tails cut off, and that Bertie, prince of Wales, was the first to wear a true dinner jacket, in that same decade. No one disputes that it was Bertie's grandson David, the one who would become the duke of Windsor, who four decades later made it acceptable and then popular. And with his success, dressing for dinner for an ordinary evening came to be regarded as semi-formal, while the tailcoat was reserved for extraordinary ones. But even in the highest circles, the practice did not survive the Second World War, after which its patrician cast was thought to offend democratic tastes. The dinner jacket then came to be worn everywhere, and the tailcoat was in Europe relegated to the grandest parties, concerts, and occasions of state, and in America to charity banquets. Thus can one see that innovations of comfort have extinguished some modes of formal wear, while improving others and marginalizing still others. And some believe that, with the rise of "business casual," dinner jackets will take the place of tails, and suits dinner jackets. But let us leave this sad exegesis covered by the veil with which it should justly be covered.

Returning to the clothes, I say that each formal garment is appropriate for wear either during the day or in the evening. And, depending on the occasion, the proper garments are either truly formal or semi-formal, as was said. The invitation should tell you which is expected. If it says "business attire" (or in Europe or Britain and its former colonies "lounge suit"), the event is informal. If it is for the evening and it specifies "white tie," it is formal; and if "black tie," semi-formal. Only the English and the Europeans specify a level of formality for daytime occasions because no one outside Europe still wears formal day clothes. And to see all four modes of formal wear done to perfection, I cannot recommend anything more highly than the old *Masterpiece Theater* production about the duke of Windsor's abdication. And everything depicted in this film—from the cut of his coats to the height and width of his wing collars to the facings on his lapels to his contemptible behavior—is correct, except that his evening formal shirts took too many studs, as will be shown. Or if you prefer American examples, the film *Philadelphia Story* depicts eminently correct day and evening formal wear, and dashing suitings to boot.

Day formal wear is almost extinct in our country, so seldom do we wear it. Yet while it is true that few of us will ever be invited to the Royal Enclosure at Ascot, most of us will get married; and if we do not get married at night, it will not be appropriate for us to wear a dinner jacket or tails. Englishmen, even those with no hope of being invited to Royal Ascot, all own formal day clothes because, in their greater sense of style, they understand that one should not idly let pass occasions to wear regal and courtly garments and so keep them on hand for weddings, to which not just grooms and groomsmen but even guests wear them. The foundation of formal day wear is the morning coat, also called the "cutaway," because its front is "cut away" from the waist, and tapered rearward as the coat descends to its bottom edge, just behind the knees. This is the coat that Kennedy wore to his inauguration, and Nixon to his daughter's wedding. It is descended from the long silk coats once worn at court. English squires took to having theirs made in buckskin, and later in heavy wool, which more suited the rigors of the country. Since they often wore them on horseback, and since they went riding mostly in the daytime, and since daylight hours all used to be called "morning," it came to be called the morning coat. In our time, it is made of suiting-weight wool and its shoulders and sleeves are tailored like a lounge suit, while the long skirt and tail recall its origins. Traditionally, it closes via two buttonholes, one on each side at the waist, joined by buttons attached with a half-inch of silk thread. Tailors call this a "link front" and in classic times it was common on all formal jackets, but today is preserved only on this coat. Morning coats always have one long center vent and peaked lapels, though in the 1930s one sometimes saw them with a notch and even with two front buttons; but one rarely does anymore, and this is one of the few sartorial improvements from classic times to our own. They are correct in either flannel for winter or worsted for summer; and either in black or gray. The former are more formal and take old-fashioned gray-and-black striped trousers, the kind that used to be worn with frock coats, called "cashmere stripes" by London tailors even though they have never been made of cashmere. They also require an odd vest, either single- or double-breasted, in pearl gray or buff. A most dandified touch for spring or summer is a vest made of buff linen. Less formal, and only appropriate for the races or a summer wedding, is the mid- or light gray morning suit with matching trousers and vest. A proper wing collar shirt and a richly woven ascot are still correct with the black coat, but have not been worn to advantage by anyone since 1939. Far more common is the turn-down collar shirt, which is correct with the black coat and required with the gray one. And these ought to have a detachable white collar; attached soft collars in white lack the presence to balance the grandeur of the coat. The body of the shirt may be some color other than white so long as it is pale and subtle, and dandies often prefer a faint stripe. If you are the groom or a groomsman, a four-in-hand wedding tie is preferred, or else solid silver; whereas guests and attendees at other occasions may enliven this somber ensemble with a more adventurous tie. Your shoes, though, must always be black, cap-toed oxfords. Broguing on the toe seam is acceptable, even preferred, but nowhere else. Traditionally, a top hat—either in black silk or the less distinguished gray felt with a black band—is worn, or at least carried. But if you go to the trouble to wear a morning coat to your wedding, you will have done your part to uphold tradition and style and can be excused for forgoing the topper.

Semi-formal day wear is sadly extinct. The last time I can remember seeing it worn was on Ronald Reagan at his first inauguration, because he judged that full formal morning dress was too haughty and might offend the people, but refused to appear at so momentous an occasion in an ordinary suit. Nonetheless, because it is so close to things we ordinarily wear, and because it is so smart that it deserves a return to favor, I shall describe it here. Semi-formal morning dress is built around the stroller, a simple, short black or dark gray coat cut like a lounge suit jacket, but always with peaked lapels and besom pockets. It is worn with black-and-white or gray striped, checked, or plaid trousers; while the odd vest, fold-collar shirt, four-in-hand tie, and shoes are identical to those worn with the morning coat, except that an attached collar looks less out of place. Traditionally, semi-formal morning dress is worn by guests to weddings, baptisms, and social occasions laden with ritual and gravity, though this tradition is dying or dead.

But semi-formal evening wear is still with us. This is what we

Americans call the "tuxedo," in honor of Lorillard, and the French and the Germans a "smoking," because of its origins as a smoking jacket. But the English name—dinner jacket and trousers—is the most proper. In our time, these garments are available in infinite modes but correct in few. First, as to color, black is always correct. How this came to be is not known, as in every former era the great (who are the arbiters of formal attire) preferred bright colors. Some trace the rise of black to a literary conceit of 19th century dandy Edward Bulwer-Lytton. The eponymous hero of his 1828 novel *Pelham* wore only black and white at night. This is said to have caught on so widely that Brummell, who always preferred blue, rebuked his black-frocked best friend by saying, "My dear Jesse, I am sadly afraid that you have been reading *Pelham*. Excuse me, but you look very much like a magpie." The more likely explanation is that the morally somber tone of the Victorian era and the soot of the Industrial Revolution (which does not show against black cloth) combined to make black the preferred color of gentlemen's town attire. And once the tailcoat became acceptable for evening wear, it carried over its black color. Later, when Victorian strictures loosened and the smokestacks belched less, men began to wear lighter colors during the day. But black remained the rule for the evening. But truly the innovation of the duke of Windsor is to be revered. For he saw that while black looks pallid under artificial light (where these garments are always worn), very dark blue looks rich and almost bottomless. And he liked the way that midnight blue dinner clothes further distinguished himself in a sea of black-clad drones. Thus he had all his evening clothes made in this color, and so do all dandies. Burgundy or dark blue or bottle green velvet are proper for true smoking jackets, which take frog- (or braided-) closures instead of buttons, and also shawl lapels, also called a "shawl collar" because the collar and lapels are one smooth, rounded swoop. Dandies will also bespeak dinner jackets made of these cloths, or possibly blackwatch tartan, for wear to private dinners in their own home or club. The most adventurous will have one in off-white for summers and tropical climes, like the jacket Bogart wore in *Casablanca*. But these alternatives should be approached with caution, for they do not command universal respect. Hardy Amies opines, "I don't suppose it matters what you wear in the Caribbean. But it looks seriously awful in Europe."

The dinner jacket is proper single- or double-breasted, but only with peaked or shawl lapels. The latter reflect the garment's origin as a smoking jacket; and, since they are proper on no other garments, they are popular with dandies, though egg-shaped men should avoid them. Ideally, shawl collar jackets should have a link front, which allows ample room for the fulsome roll of the lapels; and these should be much wider at the bottom than at the top, for skimpy shawl lapels make you appear nostalgic for the "Rat Pack" look. All single-breasted dinner jackets should have a one-button closure; the button stance on double-breasted ones should mirror that of a suit jacket, discussed at length above. Notched lapels on a dinner jacket eviscerate its formal character. As to vents, it has been wondered whether they belong on dinner jackets. If one goes back to the histories, one takes the side of those who say no, for vents originated as a sporting detail, and smoking jackets never took them, and also in the first years of the dinner jacket's ascendancy, Savile Row made it without vents. But if one turns to the reasons, one sees that side vents provide comfort and convenience with minimal disruption to the line of the garment. On the other side, one could defend a preference for no vents with recourse to reason, by appealing to the principle that evening clothes are supposed to be as simple as possible. And truly, he who discourses well on this could remain doubtful as to whether vents are correct or not. In the end, he who subtly examines the whole will draw this conclusion: no vents is most traditional and sleekest, while side vents are not incorrect. But center vents on dinner jackets are always an abomination.

Detailing is vital for formal clothes, for these impart their formal character. The lapels must be faced entirely in silk grosgrain, or if this cannot be found or for some reason you do not like it, then satin is acceptable. The buttons should all be covered with the same silk that faces the lapels. Americans also use this material for the piping on the front hip pockets (which must never have flaps); but to the English, this is a sure sign of hired clothes. The trousers must be of the same cloth as the jacket (unless the jacket is not black or midnight blue; for the trousers must always be); must not have cuffs; and their outer side seams must be covered by a long strip of the lapel facing silk. They must be cut for suspenders, for belts are anathema with formal clothes; and their waistband should never show. Thus is it decreed that single-breasted coats must be worn with either a vest or a cummerbund, a pleated sash imported by the British from India. Its folds should always face up—either, according to one tradition, to hold opera tickets, or, as the aphorism says, "to catch crumbs." Formal vests are most unlike their suiting cousins in that they are cut low in front to show your shirt studs, and often take studs themselves. Whether closed by studs or grosgrain-covered buttons, there should be three (or six if the vest is double-breasted). Peaked lapel jackets cry out for vests, while the cummerbund goes well with the shawl collar. Double-breasted jackets require neither.

A wing collar shirt is always correct, but only if made for a high, stiff, detachable collar. This must extend at least three-quarters of an inch above your jacket collar and its wings should be slightly wider than your tie, which will always be in front. In any other mode, it looks bad on everyone; when correct, it most flatters the lean and long of neck. It looks out of place with a shawl collar or a double-breasted jacket but smashing with the single-breasted peaked lapel version. Like all evening shirts, it must be white. The cuffs should be single, not double like French, yet fastened by links, not buttons; there should be a bib in front large enough to fill the expanse left exposed by the jacket; and bib and cuffs should be made from stiff, smooth cotton or else piqué (a thick, white-on-white diamond weave). The English no longer wear these shirts with black tie, but opt instead for the turn-down collar evening shirt, another comfort-born innovation of the duke of Windsor. This has a soft, pleated front, soft French cuffs, and an attached spread collar (which well complements double-breasted jackets). Dandies favor the version known as the "Marcella," which with its piqué bib, collar, and cuffs is the mean between the stiffness of the wing collar and the softness of the pleated-front shirt. Formal shirts are not buttoned but closed with studs. Dandies can always tell if your formal shirt is bespoke, because ready-made shirts take four or more studs whereas bespoke ones take only two or three, which looks cleaner and more elegant. Studs should be of some precious but not ostentatious material, such as mother-of-pearl, gold, or onyx. They need not match your cufflinks, provided these are simple and achromatic. Watches are not worn with formal wear, it being considered uncouth and rude to your hostess to check the time during an evening of jollity.

Your tie must always be a black bow. Long ties will make you look like a drug-addled actor who got lost on his way to the Academy Awards; and any color other than black like you are nostalgic for the worst excesses of the 1980s. To enliven semi-formal wear's sobriety, the English have taken to wearing brightly colored, woven silk waistcoats, reminiscent of those beloved by George IV. And in the distance of years, they have forgotten that these looked garish even on him, and in their boredom with black tie, they do not see that it also looks bad on themselves. If you want to introduce some color, much better to wear a flower in your lapel buttonhole, as Bobby Short always did.

Silk socks, the descendent of the hose worn with knee breeches at court, are best, though cotton or wool will do, but only in black. Dandies favor them with crimson clocks, so as to complement their red boutonnières. White, buff, and self (black) also make nice clocks. Three types of shoes are acceptable: velvet slippers, plaintoe patent leather oxfords, or calf pumps with silk grosgrain bows. Slippers, either monogrammed or plain, go best with smoking or unusual dinner jackets and should not be worn outside the home or club. These may be in burgundy, bottle green, or dark blue. The others must be black. The oxford goes with everything and can be worn anywhere. The pump is the last true vestige of court dress worn in our time, but since it is held to be effeminate by most men, only dandies ever wear them. They look exceptionally good with tails, which are so formal that really only these will do.

And should you ever be called on to wear a tailcoat, you must understand that its nature is to be a uniform, so that you have almost no leeway in what you may wear with it. But this should not offend you, because provided it is well made and it fits, this garment can turn any man into an Adonis, be he short or gangly, fat or lanky. You have only to see its two most excellent wearers—Fred Astaire and Duke Ellington—to understand this. Neither was particularly robust in physique, yet in their tails they always looked most excellent. And this arose from nothing other than the cut of the coat, which is such that it accentuates every potential virtue while ruthlessly suppressing every conceivable vice. The history of this coat has been discussed at length; it remains only to describe its present form. First, it is no longer truly double-breasted but cut so that it must be worn open (the better to display one's waistcoat, shirtfront, and studs); though it retains its peaked lapels and two rows of buttons (arranged like a keystone). In front it falls slightly lower than the waist, though always lower than the bottom of the waistcoat (for vest peeking out below the coat is the gravest of all white tie *faux pas*); in back the tails fall to just behind the knees. In every other respect save one it is identical to the dinner jacket and trousers (or, to say better, these are identical to it, since the tailcoat came first and semi-formal evening wear merely aspires to its elegance); and this is that instead of there being one strip of silk on the trouser seams, there are two. This is but one detail copied from the ceremonial military and heraldic uniforms worn by those entitled to them, to which the tailcoat is the civilian equivalent. This is why white tie is called "full dress" and why London tailors still call the tailcoat a "dress coat." It is always worn with a wing collar shirt, in the mode described above; a white piqué waistcoat (either single- or double-breasted) with studs or else mother-of-pearl buttons; and a white piqué bow tie—the direct descendent of Brummell's starched white linen cravats.

A dandy, therefore, will only wear formal wear in these modes, for he knows that deviations are to be avoided by one who wants to uphold tradition and to look correct and good. And he knows also that one way that the English upper class maintained the distinction between servant and served was by forcing the former to wear correct attire in incorrect combinations. Thus butlers wore black ties with tails, clerks long ties with wing collars, and footmen bow ties with morning coats and even striped trousers with tailcoats. Though butlers and footmen are rare today, they still dress like this; and no one who is not one wants to look like one. Besides, there is no reason to alter any of the modes described above. Nothing looks better than the elegant simplicity of black and white in garments that have been perfected over many decades by the best tailors and the most astute dandies. All the necessary compromises with comfort have already been made. To press further is to lapse into vulgarity for the sake not of comfort but of fashion, about which more will be said at length below. So I conclude that good formal wear must arise from good form, and that good form always requires good formal wear.

XXIV.

Why the Dandies of America
Have Lost Their Influence

When the things written above have been observed prudently, they make any man a dandy and immediately render him more stylish than if he aped the biggest stars or copied the latest magazines. For a dandy is not a slave to fashion but an avatar of style; and style changes but slowly while fashion is ever in motion. It used to be that dandies were also the arbiters and teachers of style—men with superior taste who introduced new modes and orders of dress, refined others, and dismissed still more—so that the man wishing to dress well had only to observe and imitate them. But whereas they once filled our city streets, in our time they are far fewer; and those who remain are much less observed.

And if one considers how the dandies in America have lost the influence they once wielded, one will find that a great many men have been convinced that they should not care how they dress, while among the remainder who do care some are enamored of vulgarity, others are plagued by circumstance, and still others do not know how to guard themselves against error; so that equally ill dressed are those who care and those who do not. And I say that the cause is that American tastes have been eroded by the constant tumult between the people and the great. For in every era these two diverse humors are found, which arises from this: that the people desire to ape and imitate the great, and the great desire not to be imitated by the people.

In former times, the people were deferential to the great, and though they coveted what the great deigned tasteful, they could not afford it and would not dare to wear it but wore only what was permitted to them by custom and tradition. When by chance or labor one of them came into money and tried to dress like the great, these would rebuke his insolence while his peers would ostracize him out of envy. This is well illustrated by Fielding in *Tom Jones;* and though the example therein is of women, men are no less virulent in their reaction, only less violent.

Democracy eroded the people's deference; industrialization and capitalism made them rich or not poor. No longer deferential, they ceased fearing to offend the great. No longer poor, they indulged their appetite for ostentation, imitating as best they could the modes of the great. This the great could not abide. Jealous of their monopoly on show, some used their superior wealth to trump the people, not leaving out any kind of lavish display. But even the finest clothes are within reach of all but the most impecunious of men, provided they are irresponsible. So the great had to find a new remedy. Thus did many of them, in a spectacle redolent of what the French call *nostalgie de la boue,* begin to wear garments hitherto worn only by the poorest and most wretched. These they mixed with their opulent clothes, in a manner most outrageous and unexpected, and took delight in shocking the proprieties of the people, who dared not imitate their audacity. For what the people had in money they lacked in confidence, as Steinbeck showed when he had a man of the people say to one of the great that "you got to be awful rich to dress as bad as you do." But mostly, having tasted luxury, the people were loath to return to those rags they had cast off on becoming rich. So, having no desire any longer to imitate the great, they indulged their own proclivities and created their own modes. These could not be called tasteful by any reasonable interpretation of that word.

Some still clung to the old modes, but the pressure to abandon them soon became unbearable. Among the people, these began to be despised as boring, and to dress tastefully was to risk being ridiculed as "square." Among the great, many came to believe the protestation of academics that taste was nothing but a fraud perpetrated by the great to keep down the people. Feeling guilty, they shunned those clothes denounced as tools of oppression. And this was a blow that taste could not survive. For in all societies, modes of dress are set by the great; and if they mock taste and celebrate its opposite, taste will not be held in esteem by the people, who by nature prefer kitsch.

When democracy gave way to egalitarianism, some began to complain not just that the old modes propped up unjust class distinctions, but that any standard of dress imposes conformity, stifles creativity, and suppresses individuality. Thus did they abandon any attempt to dress presentably and colored their slovenliness with the pious demand that they be judged not by how they dress but for "who they are."

Our yearning for comfort was discussed at length above. For two centuries, this natural and ordinary desire was the engine of innovation in men's dress. So long as it was constrained by considerations of taste, the results were welcome. But as taste declined, comfort asserted itself as the supreme measure of a garment's worthiness. Many men no longer consented to put up with any discomfort from their clothes but found even the smallest inconvenience intolerable. This explains the practice of wearing tracksuits in public, and also the rise of "business casual."

To the decline of American tastes in general, I wish to add one more reason why some men take no care in how they dress. And this is that they think concern for clothing is the province only of hairdressers, choreographers, interior decorators, and the like. These men fear being mistaken for one; and fear still more the possibility that affection for clothing might be a sign of something latent. But they should understand that all men wear clothes, and only fools choose to look bad. Men's tailored clothing is designed to show off to advantage the masculine form, just as women's clothes do the same for the feminine. To forgo this for fear that men's clothes will end up making you look effeminate is not reasonable. Besides this, in the annals of dress, for every Noël Coward or Lucius Beebe, there is a Clark Gable.

Yet in spite of all the difficulties, many men continue to wish to dress well and with style. That they do not is not their fault, but is sometimes the fault of circumstance, sometimes of lack of education. The most difficult circumstance of all is the dearth of first-rate dandies in the public eye. For, in having no examples to follow, men are less able to learn how to dress well. In the 1930s, dandies were everywhere. And even if a man had no occasion to see them in person, he could see them in the cinema, as all the top film stars dressed impeccably. But he who imitates the actors of today learns his ruin rather than his dandification. About the best he can look to are television newsmen, a few of whom know what they are doing. Brokaw is the most elegant, as was said. Rather's clothes fit well, but he is so slavish in aping his hero Edward R. Murrow—even patronizing the same Savile Row tailor—that he cannot be said to have any style of his own. Jennings' clothes were obviously expensive, but his choice of patterns unfortunate and his ability to assemble stylish ensembles limited. Ted Koppel dresses well but ubiquitously in blue, which betrays a lack of imagination. Stone Phillips and Matt Lauer dress with some style, though Phillips has the better tailor. John Roberts thought that dressing like Rather would help him get Rather's job, and he had reason to think so, as he saw it work for Brian Williams; yet in his case it failed.

Making things worse is the difficulty of finding decent clothes to buy even if you know what looks good. There used to be two or three bespoke tailors of repute in every American city larger than a hamlet, and dozens in each of the great metropolises. But today only New York is served by more than two, and few other cities can claim even one. And the great college towns, those erstwhile breeding grounds of style which used to support legions of delightful haberdasheries, now could not sustain even a mail order business. This is owing to the reasons given above; for, American tastes having declined precipitously, there is no longer sufficient demand to maintain all those shops and tailors.

Good off-the-peg clothing can still be found, but its purveyors are few. The stuff that is readily available everywhere is not good, because when mass marketing anything it always pays to appeal to the lowest common denominator, and in our time that is low indeed. In addition, the cost to make quality garments has risen while the cost of most everything else has declined. Men resent paying more for clothes when they pay less for food, cars, electronics, and other goods, and most clothing manufacturers have responded by cutting their costs and slashing their prices. This is done at the expense of quality; but when a man who does not understand quality sees similar looking garments that vary widely in price, he will prefer the cheaper garment and think it ridiculous that anyone would allow himself to get rooked for the more expensive. For, as the poet has written, "There is hardly anything in the world that some men cannot make a little worse and sell a little cheaper and the people who consider price alone are that man's lawful prey." So the man who both understands quality and wants to dress well has no alternative but to scour the earth for good clothes. And if he is patient and learns where to look, he can do well.

But let us come to those errors to which so many men are prone. I say that the two most common and most damaging are the beliefs that dressing well necessitates "making a statement" or else attiring oneself according to the latest fashions. Many have observed that nature has so ordered the animal kingdom that the male of most species is more highly adorned than the female. Thus we see peacocks strut their brilliantly colored tail feathers;

he-lions proudly shake their manes; and deer, caribou, moose, and the like preen over their antlers—all to reinforce hierarchies and attract mates. Some have speculated that this trait is common to males of all species, and that it accounts for the wearing of loud and garish clothes. Whether or not this is true, many men have a strong desire to set themselves apart from their peers, which impels them to adopt modes that should never even be considered. This desire was inflamed in the years following the Second World War, when fashion magazines and the garment industry conspired to push what they called "The Bold Look," a mishmash of startling colors, overwrought patterns, and funky silhouettes. Weary of wartime austerity, American men embraced it with gusto, only to abandon it when they came to fear that the Europeans did not take them seriously. And though the center of world affairs had shifted inexorably from Paris and London to New York and Washington, nonetheless American men could not bear thinking that some European held him in contempt because of his clothes. Thus the subsequent decade saw the adoption of the most sedate clothing the world has ever seen, at least on the backs of the great. Yet some never shook their affection for the bold look, and stuck with it in one form or another, helping fuel such sartorial tragedies as the Peacock Revolution of the 1960s, the universal collapse of taste in the 1970s, and the designer rage of the 1980s.

But to set oneself apart from the generality of men, it is sufficient merely to dress well, and this precludes garishness. I can do no better than to quote Boyer: "The Fred Astaires and dukes of Windsor and Douglas Fairbankses of this world would never think of wearing anything but the most proper gray flannel suits and navy blazers. Not for Cary Grant are the Day-Glo bow tie, fruit salad jewelry, or lime green dinner jacket. But who would disagree that each man possessed a singular, stylish aura?" What made them stylish was the attention they paid to every minute detail. Every part of every ensemble was thought through, with no one part, or at most one, being allowed to overshadow the harmonious whole. The difference between the appearance of these men and the vulgar was vast; but that between them and the ordinarily attired was subtle and caused less by bold patterns and bright colors than by perfect fit, rakish silhouette, quality materials, and impeccable workmanship. In all things, they adhered to the maxim of Brummell that "If Joe Blow turns round to look after you, you are not well dressed but either too stiff, too tight, or too fashionable." Above all, they never fell into the error of relying too much on fashion, which has caused the ruin of so many good men, as will be shown in the following chapter.

XXV.

How Much Fashion Can Do in Sartorial Affairs and in What Mode It May Be Opposed

It is not unknown to me that many have held and hold the opinion that the world of clothing is so governed by fashion and its mavens that men cannot defend themselves with their prudence, indeed that they have no remedy at all; and on account of this they might judge that one need not sweat much over clothes but let oneself be governed by fads. This opinion has been believed more in our times because of the great variability of modes which have been seen and are seen every day, beyond every human conjecture. When I have thought about this sometimes, I have been in some part inclined to their opinion. Nonetheless, so that our free will not be eliminated, I judge that it might be true that fashion is arbiter of half our choices, but she leaves the other half, or close to it, for us to govern. And I liken her to one of those capricious winds which, when the mood suits them, flap lapels, billow out coats, blow ties hither and yon, lift hats from the head, drop them on the street; each person curses at them, everyone yields to their impetus without being able to hinder them in any regard. And yet it is not as if men, when the air is still, could not provide for them by buttoning their coats and clasping their ties so that when they blow later, their impetus is neither so wanton nor so damaging. It happens similarly with fashion, which demonstrates her power where taste has not been cultivated to resist her, and therefore turns her impetus where she knows that coats have not been buttoned to thwart her. And if you consider America, which has suffered most from these variations and whose impetuous consumers have helped fuel them, you will see a country without buttons and without any tie clasps. If it had been secured by suitable taste, as in England and Italy, either this wind would not have brought the great variations that it has, or it would not have come here.

In every era, fashion determines what may and must not be worn; and the reason we no longer wear togas, powdered wigs, or knee breeches has nothing or little to do with nature. Fashion first bestowed her favor on the suit we wear today about a century ago, when she turned up her nose at frock coats and relegated striped trousers to formal wear. When the next lucky mode catches fashion's eye, lounge suits will go the same way. But that day can be delayed if we wear them with style and avoid her excesses. Many of these were discussed at length where we spoke of designer suits. Others pertaining to color and pattern and fabric should also be spurned with contempt. For these are introduced by designers and retailers not for the sake of making you look good but in order to make you think your clothes are obsolete so that you are seized with the desire to buy new ones. And although women are more susceptible to this than men, men are not above gullibility, as Gay Talese shows when he has a wily village tailor trick a world-weary mafioso into accepting trousers with slashed knees by telling him that they are the latest big city fashion. In general, stay only with those modes I have praised above. For although modes of dress are conventional, what looks best within them is not. In all aesthetic endeavors, the human eye can distinguish between a given mode done well or done badly. And this is why we may see two houses side by side that are both neoclassical, yet one may look harmonious and lovely while the other is gaudy and ill-formed. So too it is with clothes. To monkey with established modes for the sake of fashion is no different from doubling the entablature on the Parthenon, rebuilding Monticello out of plywood, or painting the Palazzo Strozzi hot pink.

And I wish that this may be enough to have said about opposing fashion in general. But restricting myself more to particulars, I say that one sees from time to time that some tailors and manufacturers breathe new life into old modes that have become ossified and boring, either by subtly altering silhouettes, experimenting with more lively colors and patterns, or using fabrics that are either altogether new or else seem new because they have fallen into desuetude. This is a service the Italians have been providing for more than 100 years. Back when the English aristocracy was rich and influential, one stop on the "grand tour" was Naples, because it was so near to the Pompeii ruins. The English found the clothes they had brought with them to be intolerable in the hot climate of Southern Italy. So they had new ones made, in lighter weights, by Neapolitan tailors. These tailors had been making clothes for the local indigent aristocracy for decades, but these were essentially folk costumes that bore little resemblance to the modern suit. To help the tailors understand the cut they wanted, the English would leave them a suit or two to copy. These the Neapolitans took apart seam by seam and examined minutely, learning every trick of the Savile Row trade while forgetting none of their own. The new clothes they made for their English clients combined the basic English silhouette with Neapolitan refinements, and were made of cloth that was much lighter in weight and color. Soon these clothes became the rage throughout the Empire, and anyone with reputation wore them in the hotter climes. Similarly, the Romans enlivened dress in the years following the Second World War, when the firm of Brioni single-handedly invented the Continental silhouette and revived the Italian custom of favoring bright colors and unusual fabrics more suited to warm weather. Some say that Tommy Nutter—tailor-to-the-stars in Swinging '60s London—saved Savile Row from looming death with his lively reinterpretations of moribund English modes. In our time, the Neapolitans have reasserted their preeminence as the world's greatest tailors, making their distinct silhouette and spirited approach to fabric, color, and pattern chic throughout the *haute monde*. A new generation of Nutter-inspired tailor-designers, such as Richard Anderson and Andrew Ramroop, is again enlivening Savile Row. And some eminent men, such as Kelsey Grammer, David Hyde Pierce, Jon Stewart, and Matt Lauer, have shown that it is possible to dress fashionably without getting carried away, though Lauer looks better than the others because he hews a little more closely to the old modes.

But innovation much more often harms than helps. Only those innovations are helpful that lead a mode back to its beginnings. For in their beginnings, all modes of dress must have had some goodness in them, through which they first gained reputation and adherents. Because in the process of time that goodness is corrupted, unless someone intervenes to lead it back to the mark, of necessity the mode becomes camp. The beginnings of our modes can be found in the 1930s, when, after a decade or two of trial and error, the great and their tailors perfected modes which to this day redound to their glory. Thus, let a designer who wishes to be great put before himself the second decade between the two World Wars. He will see refined silhouettes, trim shoddings, and perfectly fitting shirts; he will see elegant neckwear and discreet accessories; he will see the most tasteful, subtle, and imaginative combinations of color, fabric, and pattern. He will see golden times when each man—from the rich and wellborn to the ordinary office clerk—dressed with style, because good clothes were available and affordable, standards were higher, and people cared. The greatest designers all look to this time for inspiration—not just Flusser, but also Ralph Lauren, Luciano Barbera, Garrick Anderson, and anyone interested in style.

But your goal should be to become your own designer. For just as it is contemptible in war to rely on the arms of others, so is it contemptible in dress to rely on the judgment and taste of others. Virtue consists in developing your own judgment, and honing your own taste. Women understand this, but men are content to rely on wives, girlfriends, and mothers to select and purchase their clothes. But there has never been a well-dressed man who was dressed by women; for their tastes diverge from ours; and though they may recognize what looks good when they see it on you, they cannot recognize it in stores, being by their nature drawn to the latest fashions, the quality of which was given above. So just as they will not wear clothes purchased for them by you, you should not wear clothes selected by them. Al Gore was ruined the moment he placed himself in the hands of that wardrobe consultant who advised him to wear earth tones. Similarly, you should always approach salesmen with caution, for, to the extent that they work on commission and their merchandise is constantly turning over, their interests diverge from yours. Never trust a salesman you do not know, and never if you lack knowledge of what you want and what looks good. For this is a general rule that never fails: that a man who is not wise by himself cannot be counseled well, unless indeed by chance he should submit himself to one alone to dress him in everything, who is a very prudent man. In that case he could well be, but it would not last long, because that salesman would in a short time spend all his money.

Instead you should strive to imitate the great dressers of the 1930s, who—working with their tailors, cordwainers, and shirt-makers—designed unique wardrobes for themselves, ensuring that not only would they always be stylish, but that they would never look exactly like anyone else. Among the other magnificent things that Flusser might have put into George Frazier's mouth are these words: "Neither did the triumph of the Brahmin look set my habits, nor did the Peacock Revolution change them." Through him one sees that great dressers always look the same in every fashion; and if it varies—now by exalting riotous colors, now by peddling garish silhouettes—they do not vary but always keep their habits firm so that one easily knows that fashion does not have power over them. They never confuse fashion with dandification, and embrace the former in quest for the latter, or spurn the latter for fear of the former.

I conclude, thus, that as fashion varies from season to season, those men are well dressed whose prudence enables them to resist her charms, and those who cannot resist, ill dressed. I judge this indeed, that it is better to risk being thought hidebound than to entrust yourself to fashion, because fashion is a harlot; and it is necessary, if one wants to protect oneself, to beat her back and spurn her enticements. And one sees that she will try to trick you with siren songs, exposed flesh, and blown kisses. And so always, like a harlot, she is more successful in trapping the young, because they are less cautious, more impetuous, and lack the confidence to eschew the current.

XXVI.

Exhortation to Seize Dress and to
Free It from the Vulgarians

Thus, having considered everything discussed above, and thinking to myself whether in America at present the times have been tending toward a restoration of classic modes, and whether there is matter to give opportunity to someone prudent and virtuous to reintroduce modes that would bring honor to him and good to the community of men here, it appears to me that so many things are now tending to the benefit of a restoration that I do not know what moment has ever been more apt for it. In these harsh times, when the vagaries of "business casual" confound men, who miss the structure and predictability of the old orders; when women hold them in contempt for their slovenliness; when so many doors are closed to them because of their wretched appearance—men are longing for someone to show them style and the stylish path. And if, as I said, American tastes have gone to hell, that only increases the glory, honor, and gratitude due to you for this marvelous deed. For all honor and glory accrue to those who accomplish something difficult. And what could be more difficult than to rescue an America that is shabbier than the English, haughtier than the French, more fashion-enthralled than the Italians, without style, without class, shoddy, garish, unkempt, vulgar, and enduring blemishes of every sort.

Up to now not a glimmer has shone in someone who could judge that he was worthy of the dandies of old and who could lead the restoration. So, left as if lifeless, America awaits whoever can heal our wounds, and put an end to our confusion and slovenliness, and cure us of our sores that have festered now for so long a time. One may see how we yearn for someone to redeem us from this tastelessness. Nor may one see at present anyone in whom we can hope more than in your illustrious house, which with its fortune and virtue, supported by the corporation of which it is now prince, can put itself at the head of this restoration. And though you are not American, at least you were born here, and your company has great interests here. So you have an interest in seeing America prosper as much as we have a need for sartorial guidance and inspiration. But in this time, there is no one among our own to lead us. So we look abroad to the heir of Agnelli, that great champion of elegance, to lead us out of the sartorial desert. The people would be sure to follow, for, as I have said, the great have always set the tone of their societies' manners and dress, and the corporate elite are the aristocracy of our age—rich, powerful, envied, revered, feared yet loved; everyone aspires to be one, and if they cannot, then at least to be near them or work for them.

All this is much less difficult than what Brummell managed to do; for he had to invent whole new modes, and introduce them in the teeth of furious opposition from an aristocracy of which he was not a member. You need only resuscitate old modes, and to do that you need only to summon up the habits of the lives of those discussed above. And although these men are rare and marvelous, nonetheless they were men, and they had none of your advantages. So this endeavor cannot but be successful, provided that you keep your aim on the orders of those whom I have put forth.

Thus, one should not let this opportunity pass for America, after so much time, to see our redeemer. I cannot express with what love he would be received in every boardroom, middle manager's suite, and corner store in this country. What decent American would fail to follow? What petulant fashion critic would dare oppose you? Then may your illustrious house take up this task with the spirit and hope in which just enterprises are taken up, so that thanks to its effort the appearance of this great land may be ennobled, for in the wise words of Mark Twain:

Clothes make the man.
Naked people have little or no influence in society

Notes

Acknowledgments

Page

v   "grandeur of vision . . ." Strauss, *Thoughts on Machiavelli*, p. 13.

DL

2   "in the matter of dress . . ." Cicero, *On Duties*, I.130.

I.

4   "As Xenophon wrote in his life of Cyrus . . ." Xenophon, *Education of Cyrus*, Book I, Ch. 3.17.

III.

9   "move the observer's eye . . ." Flusser, *Style and the Man*, p. 13.

11   "the scorn of the designer Hardy Amies . . ." Amies, *Englishman's Suit*, p. 29 & plate 15.

VIII.

30   "looked as if he had been poured into his clothes . . ." Wodehouse, *Very Good, Jeeves!*, Ch. 1.

33   "His smooth jowls . . ." Wolfe, *Bonfire*, p. 531.

XI

41   "In his book *Liar's Poker* . . ." Lewis, *Liar's Poker*, p. 37.

XII.

45   "the concept of fit . . ." Boyer, *Eminently Suitable*, p. 89.

45   "he makes mafiosi-type clothes . . ." Bellow, *Ravelstein*, p. 33.

47   "as big as the Holland Tunnel" Wolfe, *Kandy-Kolored*, p. 259.

50   "line, line, and line" Michael Alden, quoted from thelondon lounge.net.

XIII.

57   "dubbed this silhouette the 'power look'..." Boyer, *Eminently Suitable*, p. 203.

60   "when trying on a new jacket..." Flusser, *Style and the Man*, p. 169.

60   "anyone can make..." Boyer, *Eminently Suitable*, p. 53.

61   "likened to a waterfall" "A Tale of Two Jackets." Michael Alden, thelondonlounge.net.

62   "Updated American" Flusser, *Clothes and the Man*, pp. 30–1.

62   "the right choice . . . will haunt . . ." Flusser, *Style and the Man*, p. 7.

XIV.

65   "a well-made buttonhole . . ." Quoted slightly out of context from Wilde, "Phrases and Philosophies for the Use of the Young," published in *The Chameleon* (Oxford University student magazine), December 1894.

XV.

72   "the truly stylish man . . ." Flusser, *Style and the Man*, p. 20.

XVI.

74   "*suivre*, 'to follow'" Amies, *Englishman's Suit*, pp. ix-x.

75   "His grandson the duke of Windsor . . ." Windsor, *Windsor Revisited*, p. 50.

81   "the Federation of Merchant Tailors . . ." Geraint Smith & Madeleine Harper, *Evening Standard* (London), October 23, 1993; *et al.*

85   "he judged it necessary to enact . . ." "Brown's Staff Told to Reflect His Stylish Self." Dan Levy, *The San Francisco Chronicle*, February 3, 1996.

XVII.

87   "men rarely see their own feet . . ." Wolfe, *Bonfire*, p. 179.

87   "Wanna know if a guy is well dressed?" Quoted in Flusser, *Making the Man*, p. 49; *Clothes and the Man*, p. 98; *Style and the Man*, p. 36; *Dressing the Man*, p. 186.

89 "Flusser records that . . ." Flusser, *Clothes and the Man*, p. 101; *Style and the Man*, p. 115.

92 "The tassel loafer, denounced by George Bush as effete and elite . . ." "The Politicization of Tasseled Loafers." Neil A. Lewis, *The New York Times*, November 3, 1993; *et al.*

98 "the sort of sagging thin black socks . . ." Lewis, *Liar's Poker*, pp. 170–171.

XVIII.

101 "Think of your face as a portrait . . ." Flusser, *Style and the Man*, p. 25.

115 "enough to make Daisy Buchanan cry . . ." Fitzgerald, *The Great Gatsby*, Ch. V.

XIX.

118 "what Tom Wolfe calls 'sartorial armor' " Wolfe, *Man in Full*, pp. 527 & 552.

121 "subdued and rich, as only these bastards . . ." Wolfe, *Bonfire*, p. 588.

124 "look like a British diplomat." Wolfe, *Kandy-Kolored*, p. 261.

XX.

136 "she had its frame covered . . ." Reported in Roetzel, *Gentleman*, p. 133.

139 "as though they've been stored . . ." Boyer, *Elegance*, p. 40.

141 "Savile Row tailor Angus Cundy predicted . . ." Howarth, *Henry Poole*, p. 146.

XXI.

142 "come into the room almost before the man" Amies, *Englishman's Suit*, p. 59.

148 "As Molloy noted . . ." Quoted slightly out of context from Molloy, *New Dress for Success*, p. 115.

149 "leap out in front of shirts . . ." Wolfe, *Bonfire*, p. 164.

151–152 "The duke of Windsor used to weed through his ties ..." Windsor, *Windsor Revisited*, p. 167.

XXII.

157 "My neckcloth, of course, forms my principal care ..." Quoted in Boyer, *Eminently Suitable*, p. 111.

XXIII.

165 "Personal hygiene apart ..." Amies, *Englishman's Suit*, p. 80.

171 "My dear Jesse," Quoted in Robins, *How to Be a Complete Dandy*, p. 98.

172 "I don't suppose it matters ..." Amies, *Englishman's Suit*, p. 79.

XXIV.

179 "This is well illustrated by Fielding ..." Fielding, *Tom Jones*, Book IV, Ch. 8.

180 "you got to be awful rich ..." Steinbeck, *Travels With Charley*, p. 238.

183 "There is hardly anything ..." John Ruskin. Quoted in Walker, *Savile Row*, p. 7.

184–185 "The Fred Astaires and dukes of Windsor ..." misquoted slightly from Boyer, *Elegance*, p. 18.

185 "If Joe Blow turns round ..." Quoted with a minor alteration from Laver, *Dandies*, p. 21.

XXV.

188 "as Gay Talese shows ..." Talese, *Unto the Sons*, pp. 96–107.

XXVI.

195 "Clothes make the man. ..." Twain, "More Maxims of Mark," in *Mark Twain: Collected Tales, Sketches, Speeches & Essays, 1891–1910*. New York: Library of America, 1992.

Bibliography

de Alvarez, Leo Paul. *The Machiavellian Enterprise: A Commentary on The Prince.* DeKalb, Ill.: Northern Illinois University Press, 1999.

Amies, Hardy. *The Englishman's Suit.* London: Quartet Books, Ltd., 1994.

Angeloni, Umberto. *The Boutonniere: Style in One's Lapel.* New York: Universe/Vendome Press, 2000.

Beerbohm, Max. "Dandies and Dandies," in *The Works of Max Beerbohm.* London: John Lane, 1896.

Bellow, Saul. *Ravelstein.* New York: Viking, 2000.

Boyer, G. Bruce. *Elegance: A Guide to Quality in Menswear.* New York: W. W. Norton & Company, Inc., 1985.

————. *Eminently Suitable: The Elements of Style in Business Attire.* New York: W. W. Norton & Company, Inc., 1990.

————. *Fred Astaire Style.* New York: Assouline, 2005.

Bridgland, A. S. *The Modern Tailor, Outfitter, and Clothier.* London: Caxton House, 1936.

Bulwer-Lytton, Edward. *Pelham, or Adventures of a Gentleman.* London: Henry Colburn, 1828.

de Buzzaccarini, Vittoria. *Elegance and Style: Two Hundred Years of Men's Fashions.* Milan: Lupetti & Co., 1992.

————. *Men's Coats.* Modena, Italy: ZanfiEditori, 1994.

Cabrera, Roberto and Patricia Flaherty Meyers. *Classic Tailoring Techniques: A Construction Guide for Men's Wear.* New York: Fairchild Publications, 1983.

Carroll, Lewis. *Through the Looking-Glass and What Alice Found There.* London: Macmillan and Co., 1872.

Chaille, François. *The Book of Ties.* Paris: Flammarion, 1994.

————. *The Little Book of Ties.* Paris: Flammarion, 2001.

Chenoune, Farid. *Brioni.* New York: Universe/Vendome Press, 1998.

Cicero, Marcus Tullius. *On Duties*. Edited by M. T. Griffin and E. M. Atkins. Cambridge: Cambridge University Press, 1991.

Croonborg, Frederick T., *The Blue Book of Men's Tailoring*. New York: Croonborg Sartorial Company, 1907.

Cucinello, Maria. *Marinella, Napoli*. Milan: Modadori Electa S.p.A., 2004.

Fielding, Henry. *The History of Tom Jones, a Foundling*. London: A. Millar, 1749.

Fitzgerald, F. Scott. *The Great Gatsby*. New York: Charles Scribner's Sons, 1925.

Flusser, Alan. *Making the Man: The Insider's Guide to Buying and Wearing Men's Clothes*. New York: Simon & Schuster, 1981.

————. *Clothes and the Man: The Principles of Fine Men's Dress*. New York: Villard Books, 1985.

————. *Style and the Man: How and Where to Buy Fine Men's Clothes*. New York: HarperCollins, 1996.

————. *Dressing the Man: The Art of Permanent Fashion*. New York: HarperCollins, 2002.

Frazier, George. "The Art of Wearing Clothes." *Esquire*, September, 1960.

Gieve, David W. *Gieves & Hawkes: 1785–1985*. Portsmouth, U.K.: Gieves & Hawkes, 1985.

Girtin, Thomas. *Makers of Distinction: Suppliers to the Town & Country Gentleman*. London: Harvill Press, 1959.

Harrison, E. P. *Scottish Estate Tweeds*. Elgin, Morayshire, Scotland: Johnstons of Elgin, 1995.

Hochswender, Woody and Kim Johnson Gross. *Men in Style: The Golden Age of Fashion from Esquire*. New York: Rizzoli, 1993.

Howarth, Stephen. *Henry Poole: Founders of Savile Row; The Making of a Legend*. Devon, U.K.: Bene Factum Publishing, Ltd., 2003.

Keers, Paul. *A Gentleman's Wardrobe: Classic Clothes and the Modern Man*. London: Weidenfeld & Nicholson, 1987. American edition: New York: Harmony Books, 1988.

Laver, James. *Dandies*. London: Weidenfeld & Nicholson, 1968.

Lenius, Oscar. *A Well-Dressed Gentleman's Pocket Guide*. London: Prion Books Ltd., 1998.

Lewis, Michael. *Liar's Poker: Rising Through the Wreckage on Wall Street.* New York: W. W. Norton & Company, Inc., 1989.

Machiavelli, Niccolò. *The Prince.* Translated by Harvey C. Mansfield, Jr. Chicago: University of Chicago Press, 1985; Second Edition, 1998.

————. *Florentine Histories.* Translated by Laura F. Banfield and Harvey C. Mansfield, Jr. Princeton, N.J.: Princeton University Press, 1988.

————. *Discourses on Livy.* Translated by Harvey C. Mansfield, Jr. and Nathan Tarcov. Chicago: University of Chicago Press, 1996.

Malossi, Giannino (editor). *Apparel Arts: La Moda è la Notizia.* Turin: Gruppo GFT, 1989. Published in the United States as *Apparel Arts: 1931/39.* New York: Architecture and Urbanism, 1992.

Mansfield, Harvey C., Jr. *Machiavelli's New Modes and Orders: A Study of the Discourses on Livy.* Ithaca, N.Y.: Cornell University Press, 1979. Reissued: Chicago: University of Chicago Press, 2001.

————. *Machiavelli's Virtue.* Chicago: University of Chicago Press, 1995.

Mayle, Peter. *Acquired Tastes.* New York: Bantam, 1992. Chapters 1, 5, & 15.

Molloy, John T. *New Dress for Success.* New York: Warner Books, 1988.

Mosconi, Davide and Riccardo Villarosa. *The Book of Ties.* London: Tie Rack Ltd., 1985.

Poulin, Clarence. *Tailoring Suits the Professional Way.* Peoria, Ill.: Chas. A Bennett Co. Inc., 1953; Second Edition, 1973.

Robins, Stephen. *How to Be a Complete Dandy: A Little Guide for Rakes, Bucks, Swells, Cads and Wits.* London: Prion Books Ltd., 2001.

Roetzel, Bernhard. *Gentleman: A Timeless Fashion.* Cologne: Könemann, 1999.

Schoeffler, O. E. and William Gale. *Esquire's Encyclopedia of 20th Century Men's Fashions.* New York: McGraw-Hill, 1973.

Steinbeck, John. *Travels With Charley In Search of America.* New York: Viking Penguin, Inc., 1962.

Steinberg, Neil. *Hatless Jack: The President, the Fedora, and the History of an American Style.* New York: Plume, 2004.

Stote, Dorothy. *Men Too Wear Clothes.* Philadelphia: J. B. Lippincott, 1939.

Strauss, Leo. *Thoughts on Machiavelli*. Glencoe, Ill.: The Free Press, 1958; Chapters I & II.

Talese, Gay. *Unto the Sons*. New York: Knopf, 1992.

Thackeray, William Makepeace. *The History of Pendennis: His Fortunes and Misfortunes; His Friends and His Greatest Enemy*. London: Bradbury & Evans, 1848–50.

Vass, László and Magda Mólnar. *Handmade Shoes for Men*. Cologne: Könemann, 1999.

Villarosa, Riccardo and Giuliano Angeli. *The Elegant Man: How to Construct the Ideal Wardrobe*. New York: Random House, 1990.

Walker, Richard. *The Savile Row Story: An Illustrated History*. London: Prion Books Ltd., 1988. American edition: New York: Rizzoli, 1989.

Waller, Jane. *A Man's Book: Fashion in the Man's World in the 20s and 30s*. London: Duckworth, 1977.

Waugh, Norah. *The Cut of Men's Clothes: 1600–1900*. London: Theatre Arts Books, 1964.

Windsor, duke of. *A Family Album*. London: Cassell, 1960. Published in the United States as *Windsor Revisited*. Boston: Houghton Mifflin, 1960.

Wodehouse, P. G. *Carry On, Jeeves*. London: Herbert Jenkins, 1925.

———. *Very Good, Jeeves!* London: Herbert Jenkins, 1930.

Wolfe, Tom. "The Secret Vice," in *The Kandy-Kolored, Tangerine-Flake Streamline Baby*, pp. 254–261. New York: Farrar, Straus and Giroux, 1965.

———. *The Pump House Gang*. New York: Farrar, Straus and Giroux, 1968.

———. "Funky Chic," in *Mauve Gloves & Madmen, Clutter & Vine*, pp. 197–215. New York: Farrar, Straus and Giroux, 1976.

———. *The Bonfire of the Vanities*. New York: Farrar, Straus & Giroux, 1987.

———. *A Man in Full*. New York: Farrar, Straus & Giroux, 1998.

Xenophon. *The Education of Cyrus*. Translated by Wayne Ambler. Ithaca, NY: Cornell University Press, 2001

Index

*References are given by chapter number (Roman)
and page number (Arabic)*

Index

herringbone, III 9; XIV 68; XVI 81, 82; XVII 98; XVIII 111; XX 134; XXII 158. *Cf.* pattern

hobbits, XX 137

Holland, XVI 74

Hollywood, VI 25; XIII 59; XIX 125, 127. *Cf.* California

homburg, XXII 160. *Cf.* hats

hopsack, XX 137. *Cf.* cloth

horizontal stripes, V 20; XVIII 113. *Cf.* shirtings

horses, VI 22; XIII 58; XVII 91, 93; XX 135; XXII 161; XXIII 165, 168. *Cf.* hunting

houndstooth, XVI 81, 82; XX 133, 134. *Cf.* pattern

Huddersfield, England, XVI 80

Hudson River Valley, XIX 126

Huguenots, XXI 148. *Cf.* French, the

Hume, Brit (1943–), television journalist and anchor; wears great pocket squares, V 21; XXII 157

Humpty Dumpty, children's nursery rhyme character immortalized by Lewis Carroll; made spectacular omelets for the White King's soldiers, VIII 31

Hungarians, the, XVII 91, 97

hunting, V 19; XIII 58; XX 135, 137; XXI 143. *Cf.* horses; leisure; squires

hunting pink, XX 137. *Cf.* color

Hustler, The (film; 1962), VIII 33

Ictinus (ca. 5th century B.C.), most celebrated architect of the ancient world; designed the Parthenon (*cf.*), X 39

image consultants, V 20; XV 71

incroyables, XX 130

India, XX 131; XXIII 173

Industrial Revolution, VI 22; XXIII 171; XXIV 179

industry, the (clothing), IV 15; VII 27; IX 35, 36; XII 46, 48; XVI 79, 80; XVII 96, 97, 98; XVIII 101, 108; XIX 125; XXI

144; XXIII 164; XXIV 183, 184; XXV 188. *Cf.* department stores; designers; fashion; salesmen

informality, XVI 83; XVII 90, 91, 98; XVIII 101–102, 105, 110; XIX 119, 128–129; XX 135, 139; XXI 146; XXIII 167. *Cf.* causal; formality

investment bankers, XVIII 113; XIX 121; XXII 156

invitations, XXIII 167

Ireland, XVII 94; XX 134

Irish poplin, XXI 144. *Cf.* ties

irregularities (of body); *see* deformities

Italian (style), XIII 57; XVII 96–97, 99; XVIII 109; XXI 147; XXII 154, 155; XXV 189

Italians, III 11; XII 47, 53, 54; XIII 61; XVI 78, 79; XVII 89, 94, 95, 96, 98; XVIII 102, 107, 111; XIX 121, 122; XX 137; XXI 145; XXII 162; XXV 188; XXVI 194. *Cf.* Milanese; Neapolitans; Romans

Italy, XII 53; XVI 78; XVIII 105, 107, 109; XXV 187, 189. *Cf.* Biella; Milan; Naples; Pompeii; Rome

Ivy League (style), XIII 55; XVII 94; XVIII 102. *Cf.* American (style); Brahmin look; Brooks Brothers; J. Press; Northeast; "trad"

J. Press, retailer; keeper of the "trad" flame, XIII 56

jacket length, III 8, 11; V 19, 21; X 38; XII 49

jacketings, XX 132, 135; XXII 161. *Cf.* cotton; flannel; hopsack; linen; odd jackets; serge; silk; tweed

jackets; *see* blazers; dinner jackets; leather jackets; Norfolk jackets; odd jackets; suits; tweed jackets

jackets (construction), IX 35; XIV 66–67. *Cf.* detailing

jackets (cut), DL 2; IV 16; VII 27, 29; VIII 31, 33; IX 35–36; XII–XIII *passim;* XIV 64. *See also* silhouette;

215

McQueen, Steve (1930–1980), actor and avatar of cool, XVI 75; XX 141

medallion (shoe toe decoration), XVII 94

medals, XIII 58; XXII 163

Meet the Press, television political talk show, XVIII 101

Menjou, Adolphe (1890–1963), film star and clothes horse, VI 25

Merino sheep, XVI 79. *Cf.* wool

Middle East, the, XVIII 105

midnight blue, XVIII 111; XIX 118; XXIII 171, 173. *Cf.* color

Milan, XIII 62; XIX 122. *Cf.* Italy

Milanese, the, XVIII 107; XIX 121, 122. *Cf.* Italians

military (institution), XIII 58; XX 138

military (look), XII 46; XIII 57. *Cf.* silhouette

Military (silhouette), XIII 58; XIV 66

military uniforms, XIII 58; XXIII 165, 176

moccasins, XIX 120

mohair, XVI 77, 84; XIX 122. *Cf.* suitings; summer suitings

moleskin, XX 136. *Cf.* cotton; odd trousers

Molloy, John T. (1936–), author and pioneer of "scientific" research to prove that conservative clothes are safer for business wear, XXI 148. *Cf.* scientific approach to dress

money, DL 1–2; V 20; VII 29; XII 52; XIV 64, 68; XXIV 179, 180; XXV 191. *Cf.* cost (of clothes); liberality; old money (look); thrift

monk straps, XVII 92, 95; XIX 118; XX 140. *Cf.* shoes

monochromatic look, VI 24. *Cf.* Grant, Cary; Philbin, Regis

Monticello, self-designed home of Thomas Jefferson, XXV 188

Monticristi, XXII 161. *Cf.* Panama hats

morning; *see* daytime

morning coats, XX 131; XXIII 168–169, 170, 177. *Cf.* formal day wear

mother-of-pearl, XVIII 109; XXIII 174–177

mothers, XIX 117; XXV 191. *Cf.* women

movies; *see* actors; films

Murrow, Edward R. (1908–1965), stepfather of broadcast journalism; lifelong customer of Savile Row, XXIV 182

muscular men, I 3; VI 22; VII *passim*

nailhead, XVI 81, 82, 84. *Cf.* pattern

Naples, XIII 61, 62; XIX 122; XXV 188. *Cf.* Italy; Neapolitans; tailors, Neapolitan

National Basketball League, VII 29. *Cf.* Riley, Pat

National Football League, V 19. *Cf.* Dierdorf, Dan

natural shoulders, VI 25; XII 46–47; XIII 57, 59, 61. *Cf.* shoulders, jacket

natural waist, III 9; VII 28; VIII 31; XII 49; XIII 61; XXII 154. *Cf.* rise, trouser; waist, jacket

navy (jacketings), XX 137, 138; XXIV 184

navy (suitings), XVI 82; XIX 118. *Cf.* blue (suitings); midnight blue

Neapolitan silhouette, XIII 61–62. *Cf.* *barchetta;* drape; *spalla camicia;* tailors, Neapolitan

Neapolitans, XVII 98; XVIII 107; XIX 121. *Cf.* Italians; shirts, Neapolitan; tailors, Neapolitan

neckwear; *see* ascots; ties

New Hampshire, XIX 127

New York City, XIII 58, 62; XVIII 107; XXIV 182, 184. *Cf.* Times Square

Nice, XII 53. *Cf.* France

Night Watch, The, a/k/a *The Militia Company of Captain Frans Banning Cocq and of Lieutenant Willem van Ruytenburch,* grand group portrait by Rembrandt van Rijn (1642), XVIII 101

19th century, IV 15; VI 22; XVI 74; XVIII 105; XX 131; XXI 144; XXIII 171

Index

Index